YOMO!

YOU ONLY MISSION ONCE

A GUIDE FOR

Sister Missionaries

HANNAH SHOAF HARDY

CFI
An imprint of Cedar Fort, Inc.
Springville, Utah

© 2025 Hannah Shoaf Hardy
All rights reserved.

No part of this book may be reproduced in any form whatsoever, whether by graphic, visual, electronic, film, microfilm, tape recording, or any other means, without prior written permission of the publisher, except in the case of brief passages embodied in critical reviews and articles.

This is not an official publication of The Church of Jesus Christ of Latter-day Saints. The opinions and views expressed herein belong solely to the author and do not necessarily represent the opinions or views of Cedar Fort, Inc. Permission for the use of sources, graphics, and photos is also solely the responsibility of the author.

Paperback ISBN 13: 978-1-4621-4879-0
eBook ISBN 13: 978-1-4621-4880-6

Published by CFI, an imprint of Cedar Fort, Inc.
2373 W. 700 S., Suite 100, Springville, UT 84663
Distributed by Cedar Fort, Inc., www.cedarfort.com

Library of Congress Cataloging Number: 2025931857

Cover design by Shawnda Craig
Cover design © 2025 Cedar Fort, Inc.
Edited by Liz Kazandzhy

Printed in the United States of America

10 9 8 7 6 5 4 3 2 1

Printed on acid-free paper

*This book is dedicated to all young women everywhere.
God believes in you and loves you.*

Contents

Preface 1
Introduction: Why I Chose to Serve a Mission 4
1   The Worth of Souls 10
2   Be *You* 20
3   Dealing with Perfectionism 32
4   Joy 42
5   Having Fun on Your Mission 58
6   Trusting Heavenly Father 63
7   Divine Help 72
8   Serving before Flirting 83
9   Don't Give Up 90
10 The Power of Agency 98
11 Service Saves Souls 105
12 Working with Members 114
13 Always Strive to Follow the Spirit 121

14	All about Companions 130
15	Sources of Support 138
16	How to Prepare Physically, Mentally, Emotionally, Spiritually, and Socially 145
17	How to YOMO After Your Mission 168
18	Blessings from Serving 174

Appendix A: History of the Germany Berlin Mission and the Freiberg Temple 181

Appendix B: Glossary 187

Acknowledgments 189

About the Author 192

PREFACE

Dear readers,

You're probably wondering why this book is titled YOMO. YOMO means "you only mission once," and it's the missionary version of YOLO (you only live once). While we all "mission" throughout our lives, sharing the gospel of Christ as members of His restored Church, this book focuses specifically on young full-time missionaries. YOMO is about living your mission to the fullest by joyfully serving, being focused on the work, being fearless in sharing the gospel, and having fun. Also, this book addresses the needs, worries, and concerns specific to *sisters* (one of the best kinds of missionaries there are!—but I guess I'm biased). It's for sisters who know they want to serve and for sisters who may still be deciding whether to serve or not. I hope my story can help you as you prayerfully decide what's right for you.

The reason I wrote this book about how to YOMO is because I did the complete opposite for far too long on my mission. Fear, doubt, and concerns about what other people thought of me weighed me down. I wasn't fully present in the moment. But when I learned to rely more on Christ, everything changed. The more I trusted the Lord, the more I could serve with faith, love, and confidence.

I hope to inspire you to be more prepared for your missions than I was so that you can YOMO more easily. With the focus on "you only mission once," I hope to show you how missionary work can be fun while also respecting the reverence of the call to serve. While my advice is geared toward missionaries, young women can apply these principles both in and out of the mission field.

The principles and advice in YOMO come from my personal experience (and many mistakes!) serving in the Germany Berlin Mission. While there is so much information I'm excited to share with you to help you prepare for your own service, I don't claim to have all the answers about missionary work because there is only One who does: the Lord, whose work is "to bring to pass the immortality and eternal life of man" (Moses 1:39).

I want to make a confession: I was *not* a perfect missionary! Perfect missionaries don't exist. Only the Savior was perfect, so please don't put the pressure of missionary-perfectionism on yourself. This book of advice doesn't come from a sister who had it all figured out but from a sister who struggled and changed and struggled again—from a sister who didn't have all the answers but who learned how to rely on One who does, and who, after lots of tears and growth, was able to enjoy the work and YOMO!

Throughout this book, I intentionally use the word *strive*, meaning "to devote serious effort or energy, endeavor" or "to struggle in opposition, contend"[1] to emphasize that you don't have to be perfect—you just need to keep trying. Striving means giving your best effort and even struggling before improving. Whenever I use the word *strive*, I want you to remember that the Lord doesn't expect flawlessness and will reward your incremental improvements.

To all of you young women out there, I hope my story gives you greater courage, strength, comfort, and peace. God loves you. *You are enough.* You are good enough to serve a mission. It's not so much about your abilities as it's about your heart and resolve, but I promise—you have talents and skills that God and His children need! Also, know that your mission will be different than mine and anyone else's. You will have different experiences and trials. But please know that

---

1. *Merriam-Webster.com Dictionary*, s.v. "strive," accessed July 23, 2024, https://www.merriam-webster.com/dictionary/strive.

the Lord offers you the same joy and peace He offers to all who serve Him (see Alma 26:27; John 14:27).

If anything in my little book inspires you, hold on to it. Most importantly, listen to the Spirit's inspiration that will be personally and perfectly tailored to you. Stay close to the Lord, and He will stay close to you (see Doctrine and Covenants 88:63). Serve with all your heart, might, mind, and strength (see Doctrine and Covenants 4:2). YOMO the heck out of your mission! The world needs *you*, and what you can offer is unique and so important!

Your YOMO Guide,
Hannah

INTRODUCTION
WHY I CHOSE TO SERVE A MISSION

Many sisters wonder about whether they should serve a full-time mission. Even though every young woman has a different experience, I hope that by sharing my backstory, it will help you navigate your own decision process more smoothly.

It was my first year of college—finally! Earlier that year, my parents had urged me to apply to multiple colleges, but there was only one school I wanted to hear back from: Brigham Young University (BYU). When acceptance letters from other colleges came in the mail, I would calmly open the envelope, glance at the letter, and set it back down on the kitchen counter. But when BYU's letter finally came in the mail, I ripped open the envelope and announced to my family and friends that I was going to Provo! That August, my parents and younger siblings traveled with me to Utah to drop me off at my on-campus dorm.

During my freshman year at BYU, I was blessed with amazing roommates and a fun group of young women in my Young Single Adult (YSA) ward. While I spent most of my time studying (I was such a nerd), I also enjoyed the social scene—like eating delicious maple-doughnut "Cougar Tails" with my friends while watching intense soccer matches and jamming out to pop music with my roommates during gymnastics meets. Everything about campus and student life was new and exciting!

There was just one area that was challenging to me: dating. In high school, I was shy and rarely interacted with boys. I was excited about dating my first year of college, but to my dismay, I didn't date much. I was so awkward with boys! For example, one afternoon, I was leaving my English class when one of my classmates—who I found quite attractive—wanted to walk with me. As he talked to me, I gathered my books to my chest and shyly looked at the ground the whole time. I blew that opportunity! Or there was the time when I was studying for a test, and the cutest boy from my social dance class wanted to walk with me to class, but I told him no because I was determined to finish reading the section in my textbook before class. Only years later did I realize I had missed a perfect opportunity. (#datingfails)

Along with dating, missions were a hot topic at BYU. In 2012, when I was in high school, President Thomas S. Monson announced that sisters could serve missions at age nineteen instead of age twenty-one.[2] Ever since then, more and more young women had been serving missions. Some of my friends started filling out their papers. I, however, hadn't made plans to serve.

When I was younger, I enjoyed having the sister missionaries over for dinner. As they shared their testimonies, I felt the Spirit, and they seemed to have a spiritual glow about them. After one such visit when I was fifteen, I wrote in my journal that I wanted to serve. But as I grew older, a mission was no longer on my radar—I just wanted to focus on school. However as I watched my friends open their mission calls and accept the call to serve, I began to once again consider serving.

During my second semester of college, I started thinking more seriously about my future. I didn't know what steps to take next, and the months ahead seemed like a giant blank slate. I would often sit on the green lawn next to the duck pond near Heritage Halls and

---

2. "President Thomas S. Monson Announced A Lower Age Requirement for Missionary Service," newsroom.ChurchofJesusChrist.org.

contemplate the various paths I could go down. I studied the scriptures and prayed about what direction to take next, trying to decide between serving a mission, studying abroad, or continuing my college education. As I read the scriptures, the Spirit confirmed to me the importance of missionary work. But I was also filled with peace and excitement as I considered applying for an English Language study-abroad program in Great Britain.

When freshman year ended, I flew home to Indiana to work and save more money for college. My internal debate about the future continued. I remember escaping to the creek outside my grandma's house one Sunday to mull over my decisions in a private and peaceful location, sitting underneath a leafy canopy next to the gurgling stream. Although I didn't come to a conclusion that afternoon, I felt reassurance from the Holy Ghost. Every time I prayed, pondered, and pored over the scriptures, the Spirit quietly prompted me to serve a mission. Yet every moment that I was left to my own thoughts, away from my personal study time, fear and doubt began to creep in. Could God be really prompting me to serve a mission? Leaving home and family, following a strict schedule, talking to strangers every day . . . it sounded so hard and overwhelming.

I was frustrated as I tried to make a decision that summer. Looking back, I realize I just wanted God to decide for me. I wanted Him to tell me through some huge, unmistakable spiritual impression that I needed to serve a mission. However, a loud declaration never came. Instead, I received peaceful invitations to move forward—quiet promptings that serving a mission would be a good thing. Finally, near the end of the summer, I decided I wanted to go. I asked Heavenly Father if my decision to serve was the right choice for me, and I felt the Spirit strongly, a burning in my heart, that yes, I *should* move forward and submit my mission papers. A few weeks later, I did. My parents were surprised that I wanted to serve a mission (I think my mom thought I'd choose to study abroad), but they supported me.

Waiting for my mission call to arrive during my third semester at BYU felt as painstakingly slow as a red traffic light when you're running late. But finally, my call arrived, and I mustered the patience to wait until the evening to read it, with my family watching online and my roommates supporting me in person. In our tiny apartment, I opened the letter and read, "You are assigned to labor in the Germany Berlin Mission." My mouth dropped. I was shocked. The crazy thing was that I had prayed to serve in Germany! I had taken German classes in high school, and my amazing teacher caused me to fall in love with the culture and the language. I had daydreamed many times about exploring cities with cobblestone streets and curtsying in castles. I couldn't believe that I was going to serve in Germany! My roommates and family were excited for me, and I was beyond happy. (No, you don't always get to serve where you pray to serve, but I'm grateful that ended up being the case for me!)

After I opened my mission letter, I mentally checked out from student life. I dreamt about Germany and was eager to begin my life as a missionary. But still, I had to finish my third semester first, and that wasn't easy. I believe Satan sent challenges my way to cause me to stumble and doubt serving a mission. However, staying close to the Lord in prayer—and not doubting the confirmation I received from the Lord that serving was right for me—helped me overcome challenges. I completed my classes and spent two months at home in Indiana before reporting to the Preston England Missionary Training Center (MTC) in February 2016. (Honestly, I probably spent too much time relaxing and not enough time preparing those last couple of months, but it was good to spend that time with my family before I left).

Being set apart and preparing to leave home felt so surreal. I was about to embark on the greatest opportunity of my life so far. My stomach was in knots, and I was beyond nervous, but I was excited to serve a mission and share the joy I had and still have because of the gospel of Jesus Christ. (I must confess that I also wanted an adventure and was excited to travel, although that wasn't necessarily the best reason.) I had decided to serve, knowing that the Spirit had prompted me and God had confirmed my choice. As President Dieter F. Uchtdorf has told us sisters, "Your 'once upon a time' is now,"[3] and my time to serve had arrived!

---

3. Dieter F. Uchtdorf, "Your Happily Ever After," *Ensign* or *Liahona,* May 2010, 127.

YOMO Truths: Before You Step Into the MTC

1. **Deciding to serve.** Serving a mission is a very personal decision. You don't have to go just because your friends do or because it's culturally accepted and praised. Serve a mission because you want to share the joy you have felt living the gospel of Jesus Christ. Accept the call to be a full-time missionary because you have prayed about it and feel peace about your decision.

    If you want to serve and God shows you another path, know that He loves you and has great things in store for you. If you decide to go on a mission and have to come home early for whatever reason, know that Heavenly Father values your service and sacrifice and loves you. Also, if as a missionary you make mistakes and fall short of your own goals at times, like we all do, please know that the Lord accepts your offering (see Hebrews 6:10) and that you don't have to do everything perfectly to have served a worthy mission.

2. **Where you serve.** Sisters, regarding where you serve, I'd like to point out that the Apostles call each missionary to a specific area and country by divine inspiration. Many missionaries get called to places they don't expect. While I presumptuously prayed for Germany and may show some bias throughout this book toward Europe (since I loved living there so much), I want you to know that every country and every mission is important because God loves His children everywhere. Wherever you get called to serve, it'll be where you are meant to be. While I bet you'll fall in love with whichever mission you serve in, remember that it's more about *how* you serve, not *where* you serve.

3. **Being set apart.** When I was set apart to be a missionary, I remember feeling that a special mantle, a sacred responsibility, was placed upon me. As the first chapter in *Preach My Gospel* teaches, missionaries are set apart to teach the gospel of Christ

with authority.[4] This applies to sisters as well as elders, as President Dallin H. Oaks taught, "We are not accustomed to speaking of women having the authority of the priesthood in their Church callings, but what other authority can it be? When a woman—young or old—is set apart to preach the gospel as a full-time missionary, she is given priesthood authority to perform a priesthood function."[5]

I wish to emphasize this point: As a missionary, you are set apart with priesthood authority! As *Preach My Gospel* explains, with this authority "comes the right, privilege, and responsibility to represent the Lord and teach His gospel."[6] When you serve and teach as a missionary, you have the authority of the priesthood to act in the Lord's name. Additionally, as President Spencer W. Kimball taught, being set apart in the Church means being "*set apart* from the world."[7] When I was set apart by my stake president, I did feel different. I felt the sacred duty of the call to serve.

Finally, one note about the format of this book. The following chapters contain stories from my mission, useful principles, and what I wish I had known before I served.[8] After this main section of each chapter, there are a few reflection questions and/or an activity—a call to action for readers to apply what they've learned. This is followed by a "Study Session" section, which lists scriptures, talks, and other uplifting media from leaders of The Church of Jesus Christ of Latter-day Saints on specific missionary themes. Don't feel pressured to read every reference listed, but listen to the Spirit and study a few sources that stand out to you. Throughout this book, I want you to learn with the Holy Ghost and focus on the advice that speaks to you the most.

With that, I think we're ready to begin! Let's YOMO!

---

4. *Preach My Gospel: A Guide to Sharing the Gospel of Jesus Christ* (2023), 3.

5. Dallin H. Oaks, "The Keys and Authority of the Priesthood," *Ensign* or *Liahona*, May 2014, 51.

6. *Preach My Gospel*, 3.

7. Spencer W. Kimball, as quoted in Kenneth Johnson, "Called and Set Apart to Serve," *Ensign*, June 2010, 27.

8. Please note that I use pseudonyms in the stories throughout the book.

1

The Worth of Souls

Don't let the world define your worth. Let God define it.

"You are a beloved daughter of Heavenly Father, prepared to come to the earth at this particular time for a sacred and glorious purpose."[9]

We Matter to God

My mission didn't begin when I stepped off the plane and onto German soil. It started when I was set apart and sent to the missionary training center (MTC) in Preston, England. As a basic American girl, I was eager to hear British accents. The night before I had to leave to go to the MTC, my stomach was full of fluttering butterflies and jolts of excitement. I frantically raced between my bedroom upstairs and our family's piano room downstairs, where my suitcases were partially packed. It was about 9 p.m., and I still hadn't finished packing. I totally stressed out my poor dad. So I 10/10 don't recommend waiting until the last minute to pack!

---

9. "Welcome to Personal Progress," *Young Women Personal Progress* (2009), 1, ChurchofJesusChrist.org.

The next morning, after my bags were packed and I managed to get some rest, I headed to the airport. I traveled on my first international flight with other American sisters, headed to England. The three of us sat together on the flight and developed a sisterly bond. Likely due to our collective nervousness, we found everything about the flight hilarious. Their friendship calmed my nerves about the next eighteen months of my life!

After a long but fun flight, we arrived at a British airport and drove to the England MTC. The MTC mission president and his wife greeted us, and we began our two-week missionary training. My fellow sisters-in-training were from Europe, and I loved hearing their accents.

The MTC in England was pleasant and small, with a spacious lawn and a delightful, well-trimmed garden. I enjoyed the opportunities to jog around the perfectly-trimmed bushes and the picturesque, budding flowers during exercise time. The Preston England Temple, right next to the MTC grounds, added to the beauty. It was a beacon of hope and a peaceful haven.

While my time in the MTC was full of spiritual teaching and learning, it was not without its challenges. I felt like a caged bird, dying to go outside the doors and explore the quaint British countryside. I was both eager and anxious for my departing flight to Berlin. I would ask myself, "Am I really doing this? Giving eighteen months of my life to the Lord?" Adjusting to the new missionary routine and schedule was difficult for me. I wondered, "Am I cut out for this? Am I good enough to be a missionary?" Doubt gnawed at me like a slowly creeping dementor, and waves of anxiety crashed around me, threatening to drown me in fear and panic.

During this time, my drowning didn't go unnoticed by the Lord. The Spirit sent me reassurances, reminding me why I had accepted the call to serve. One afternoon, during my favorite part of the day besides dinner—exercise time—I was doing sit-ups in the small workout room when I looked up and saw a painting that instantly touched my heart. It showed two missionaries, elders, standing next to a young boy, all dressed in white at a beach. As I gazed at the artwork, I felt the Spirit strongly and said to myself, "*This* is why I'm going on a mission and can't give up. I'm here to help another person find the joy of the gospel and feel Christ's love."

Another aid sent to comfort and strengthen me was my fellow sisters, both those who were Germany-bound like me and those sent to other places in Europe. There were only about twenty of us sisters at the MTC, and I felt blessed to have a more intimate missionary training experience than I probably would have experienced at a larger MTC. My sisters became my lifeline! During meal times, all of us would laugh and chat together. There was one sister who was always willing and eager to run with me. Also, when I was super stressed and almost burst into tears one night while praying, all the sisters huddled around me and comforted me. Their support and friendship made my stress more bearable and my MTC experience more fun.

Along with the sisters, another true disciple of Christ who lifted me up when I needed rescuing was the England MTC president. The president was very kind and observant. During one meeting with him, I was fighting to hold back the tears and anxiety rising within me like a tsunami when he asked, "How are you feeling about your mission?" I mumbled a response, and he reassured me about my service. It was not the words he shared that touched me but how he conveyed Christlike love and kindness. I felt the Spirit as he comforted me. Somehow, the president could tell I needed help, and he didn't let me fall through the cracks. He exemplified how Christ is our Shepherd, ministering to the one (see John 10:14; 3 Nephi 17:9, 21). His support and watchful care were one of the main reasons I stayed on my mission.

The final reassurance I received was in the Preston England Temple. Before my group and I flew to Germany, we got to attend one endowment session. Near the end of the session, I fervently prayed. I pleaded for answers to my doubts and concerns. As I prayed, I felt the Holy Ghost reassure and comfort me about my service, with the Lord promising me that my mission would be of great value. Armed with that strong spiritual experience and the love and support of the MTC president and my fellow missionaries, I moved forward. The next day, my Germany-destined sisters and I boarded the plane that would take us on an eighteen-month adventure that would change our lives.

YOMO Truths: Why the Worth of Souls Matters

I share these stories of comfort with you because these experiences taught me about Heavenly Father's love. He loves each of us, and you matter to Him! As President Russell M. Nelson taught in a worldwide devotional for young adults, "In all of eternity, no one will ever know you or care about you more than He does."[10] He explained how we can ask for the Lord's help and how the Spirit and angels will come to our aid.

Sisters, the prophet's words are true: Heavenly Father loves you! On your mission and throughout your life, you can turn to Him, and He will help you. He wants you to succeed. At times when I struggled on my mission, Heavenly Father sent the Spirit and earthly angels to comfort me. You can pray to and rely on Him, and He will strengthen and uplift you just as He did for me.

Heavenly Father has wondrous plans for us, beyond our understanding. Moses 1:39 speaks about this truth, and one MTC teacher instructed me to diligently study this verse. In this scripture, the prophet Moses talked to God face to face, and God told Moses, "My work and glory . . . [is] to bring to pass the immortality and eternal life of man." Isn't it amazing that Heavenly Father has a divine vision for our lives? As missionaries, we can remember that it's *His* work and glory, and because of that, we'll have His help and direction.

We matter to God, and He sees the potential in us. Dr. Kristen L. Matthews taught at a BYU devotional, "We are His children. He loves us unconditionally, eternally, and unchangingly. Our worth is infinite because we are His daughters and sons."[11] Sisters, this is what the doctrine of the "worth of souls" is all about. We all equally matter to God because He is our Father. Remember your inherent worth as His daughter and that He has a plan for you. No matter how small you feel, you are destined for greatness.

In addition to our omnipotent Heavenly Father, our Savior, the architect of the universe, also considers us to be just as precious.

---

10. Russell M. Nelson, "Choices for Eternity" (worldwide devotional for young adults, May 15, 2022), Gospel Library.
11. Kristin L. Matthews, "The Worth of Souls is Great" (Brigham Young University devotional, Aug. 6, 2013), 2, speeches.byu.edu.

Regarding the worth of souls, Doctrine and Covenants 18:10–11 teaches, "Remember the worth of souls is great in the sight of God; For, behold, the Lord your Redeemer suffered death in the flesh; wherefore he suffered the pain of all men, that all men might repent and come unto him."

I love these verses! It's empowering and reassuring to know that Jesus Christ, our Savior and Elder Brother, sees great worth in each of us, so much so that He atoned for all our sins. The Guide to the Scriptures explains that *atone* means "to suffer the penalty for an act of sin, removing the effects of sin from the repentant sinner and allowing him [or her] to be reconciled to God."[12] The Savior atoning for our sins means making us clean so that we can be reunited with our Heavenly Father. Whenever I worry too much about what the world thinks of me, it comforts me to remember that Christ sacrificed for us all, and He invites everyone to partake of His goodness and mercy. No one is excluded. Each of us has great worth because we are God's children, and His Son died for each of us.

Now, it can be easier to just read about the worth of souls than to apply it to our lives. President Nelson said that due to how frequently we learn about our identity as children of God, we may fail to miss the sacredness of that doctrine, but our identity truly matters because our understanding of who we are shapes every choice we face.[13]

While the Spirit has testified to me about the reality of our divine nature, I have been guilty of what President Nelson mentioned—of mindlessly reading or repeating the words about our true worth instead of actively internalizing and remembering that truth. It's easy to get caught up in how others define us or what the world thinks of us instead of making decisions while remembering we are children of our Heavenly Father. So how can we all internalize this great truth and believe in our divine worth more?

---

12. Guide to the Scriptures, "Atone, Atonement," Gospel Library.
13. Russell M. Nelson, "Choices for Eternity."

YOMO Tips on Internalizing Our Divine Worth

1. **Pray and ask to feel your Heavenly Father's love for you.** Sister Michelle D. Craig, in her talk "Eyes to See," encouraged us to pray for a spiritual witness of our divine identity and to ask God how He sees us individually.[14] Acting on Sister Craig's suggestion, I was reassured of my divine worth through the Spirit, and I have felt Heavenly Father's love for me. Remembering my divine worth helps me be more confident, more loving toward others, and less worried about the world's perception of me. I know that Heavenly Father loves each of His daughters equally, with a depth of unconditional love that we do not fully comprehend. Follow Sister Craig's invitation, and ask God how He feels about you. I promise you will receive an answer!

2. **Strive to focus on what God thinks of you, not what the world thinks of you.** This is not an easy thing to do, so know that you don't have to be perfect at it, but *strive* (or give an honest effort) to do so. While the world teaches us that we only matter if we're beautiful, wealthy, or score high on other mortal ideals, the gospel teaches that we matter to Heavenly Father no matter what. It's hard for me sometimes to ignore the voices of the media and other people's opinions, but the more we learn about God and His love for us, the happier and more at peace we will be with ourselves. Additionally, we can get to know Heavenly Father and His Son through scripture study and prayer, keeping us more connected to divine truths and more disconnected from worldly pressures.

3. **Make your identity as a child of God your number one identity.** In his worldwide devotional for young adults, "Choices for Eternity," President Nelson discussed the power of labels and reminded us that while we can have multiple labels, one of the most important ones to remember and hold on to is "child of God." Follow the prophet's counsel and make

---

14. Michelle D. Craig, "Eyes to See," *Ensign,* November 2020, 15–17.

"child of God" your most "important identifier."[15] Although it can be challenging, as we strive to value the things of God more than the things of this world, we will more readily be able to trust in our divine worth. This can look like spending more time studying the scriptures and less time on social media, or attending the temple more often and serving others more. We will be blessed with greater peace, confidence, and love as we pursue our divine destinies as daughters of God and followers of Christ.

As you strive to learn about and internalize your worth as a child of God (and be patient with yourself since it's a lifelong process), you will be a happier and more confident missionary. The more you feel Heavenly Father's love, the more you will want to share it with others. Remember, the doctrine of the worth of souls applies to everyone, including the people you teach, the missionaries and members you serve with, and even those who reject your message.

The Savior is our perfect example as we strive to recognize the worth of everyone around us. Jesus Christ looked past worldly labels and knew every individual's divine value. Sister Craig said, "We can follow the example of Jesus and see individuals—their needs, their faith, their struggle, and who they can become."[16] As missionaries, we can strive to be like Christ and look past appearances and see others as children of God with endless worth and potential. We can believe in people's capacity to change. As people go through trials, we can treat them with love and compassion instead of judgment. We can teach anyone willing to listen, regardless of their present-day barriers to accepting the gospel. We can also serve and love others and pray for charity to see others through Heavenly Father's eyes. As Elder Dale G. Renlund taught, "I now realize that in the Church, to effectively serve others we must see them through a parent's eyes, through Heavenly Father's eyes. Only then can we begin to comprehend the true worth of a soul."[17]

---

15. Russell M. Nelson, "Choices for Eternity."
16. Michelle D. Craig, "Eyes to See," 15.
17. Dale G. Renlund, "Through God's Eyes," *Ensign* or *Liahona*, Nov. 2015, 94.

Learning of your divine worth and striving to see people through Heavenly Father's eyes will help you be a YOMO missionary. I was able to serve more confidently and genuinely when I remembered how much God loved me and when I felt His love for the people around me. Conversely, the more I focused on myself and my flaws, the more inadequate and awkward I felt around people. But as I strove to have the Spirit with me, prayed for charity, and focused on others, I felt God's love for myself and His children in greater abundance. It was empowering and helped me YOMO.

YOMO Story: Cinderella and the Worth of Souls

I met an extraordinary sister in Chemnitz, Germany. Her name was Anisha, and she was a young American woman living in Germany. Anisha had gorgeous auburn hair, large, beautiful eyes, and a contagious personality that made you feel happier just being in her presence. During my time in Chemnitz, we became friends, and she shared with me an awesome email she had sent to her sister, who was serving a mission at the time. Using Disney's live-action movie *Cinderella*, she taught her sister about worth, envy, and service. I want to share Anisha's "Comparison is the Thief of Joy." (Many attribute this phrase to Theodore Roosevelt.)[18] She compares looking for validation from others to the Cinderella story, describing how these ideas about self-worth relate to missionary work:

> Ella's stepmother lives a life of misery, never ceasing to compare herself and her daughters to others. This jealousy eventually leads her to cruelty. After Ella's father dies, she loses the money that had helped her stay on top. Her self-worth is tied up in [being better than others], so of course it hurts.
>
> Ella's stepsisters were raised to only know their value by exterior circumstances. Isn't that the most vulnerable situation ever? When you know that you could become as good as dead if your exterior circumstances change? What a scary world to live in.

---

18. "Theodore Roosevelt | Quotes | Quotable Quote," Goodreads, accessed Nov. 15, 2023. https://www.goodreads.com/quotes/6471614-comparison-is-the-thief-of-joy.

> The stepmothers and stepsisters see Ella's innate joy and don't know how to have it. They want to crush it because they see themselves as dim in comparison even after they spend their whole lives trying to look bright.
>
> Ella knows that the exterior circumstances are clearly temporary, and she doesn't tie up her worth in them in the least. She is grateful and seeks to go see Kit [the Prince], who she knows will be her friend regardless of her attire because she came to know him at her most scraggly time. She knows he likes her for her courage and kindness, not her looks.
>
> Be a fairy godmother to your companions and investigators. This doesn't mean changing their external situations—it means helping them know that the true love of God cares nothing about exterior circumstances and everything about just giving your best. Ella had her mom's old-fashioned dress and knew it wasn't like her sisters' dresses, but it was enough to go to the ball. God loves us for who we are, at our worst and most scraggly. He sends fairy godmothers to help us remember that we have to keep believing and not give up!
>
> I'm convinced you and your companions will come upon many Ellas who have fallen on their knees and are ready to give up as she did—who stop believing. You come to them and ask for milk (figuratively speaking), and then help them see their worth.
>
> Similarly, you will come across one or two stepmothers who feel they have no self-worth beyond what they can show the world. Love [them] too, and teach them God's forgiveness.

I *love* Anisha's Cinderella-missionary story. It resonates with me because for starters, I love fairy tales and princesses *way* too much, plus I struggle with jealousy. Also, I've always imagined myself as the princess in the story, but sometimes I have a stepmother-like tendency to base my worth on external things, like beauty, productivity, and intellect. Anisha's words stick with me because she shows us how to ease the ache of envy and insecurity by applying the balm of divine love. Let us be like Ella and remember who we are: daughters of God with immutable, inherent, and eternal worth. Let us also be fairy godmothers and treat the people we meet with charity and compassion. Be an Ella and a fairy godmother on your mission, and I know you will YOMO and change lives!

Reflection Questions

1. How does knowing your worth as a child of God help you avoid envy and replace jealousy with love?

2. It can be easy to get caught up in the world's lies and believe, like the stepmother, that our worth comes from external circumstances. How can we change this way of thinking? How can we be like Ella and remember that our worth is inherent?

3. Sometimes we just need someone to remind us of our worth. How can you be a "fairy godmother" and help remind the people around you about their true worth? Or help remind the people you teach about their true worth?

Study Session: Scriptures and Talks I Love About Our Divine Worth

- Russell M. Nelson, "Choices for Eternity" (worldwide devotional for young adults, May 2022), Gospel Library.

- Dieter F. Uchtdorf, "Your Happily Ever After," *Ensign* or *Liahona*, May 2010, 124–27.

- Michelle D. Craig, "Eyes to See," *Ensign* or *Liahona*, Nov. 2020, 15–17.

- Dale G. Renlund, "Through God's Eyes," *Ensign* or *Liahona*, Nov. 2015, 93–94.

- Dieter F. Uchtdorf, "Our True Identity" (video), Gospel Library.

- "Young Women Theme," Gospel Library.

- Doctrine and Covenants 18:10–16;1 Samuel 16:7; 2 Nephi 26:33

2
BE *YOU*

Despite popular belief, you actually
don't have to be a Barbie robot.

"God made you to be you, so learn to love you."
—Jenna Lucado[19]

BEING YOURSELF *WORKS*

When I started my mission, I was convinced I needed to be some perfect Barbie missionary. You know, the type of sister missionary who is sociable, angelic, kind, service-oriented, well-mannered, poised, confident, and beautiful. While nothing is wrong with these traits, I was basically convinced that I needed to be a robot and suppress my true self. I thought that if I acted the part of the Flawless Barbie Robot Missionary, everyone would want to hear the gospel message. However, to my surprise, I learned that I was dead wrong.

In August of 2016, the sister missionaries of the Berlin Germany Mission, including me, had the opportunity to participate in the

---

19. Jenna Lucado, *Redefining Beautiful: What God Sees When God Sees You* (Nashville, TN: Thomas Nelson Inc., 2009), 133.

Freiberg Temple open house. The temple was being rededicated after its second renovation. As part of our volunteer preparation, local Church and mission leaders taught us about the miraculous history of the temple's construction in East Germany, which made serving at the open house even more humbling and remarkable. I want to share a snippet of that story with you because it's about having faith and trusting God's promises.

Local leaders gave each of us sisters a copy of David F. Boone and Richard O. Cowan's article "The Freiberg Germany Temple: A Latter-day Miracle," which outlined the noteworthy history of the temple. As Boone and Cowan explain, the state of Saxony, leading up to the building of the temple, was behind the Iron Curtain.[20] (The Iron Curtain was "a political, military, and ideological barrier" that separated western Germany from Soviet-controlled eastern Germany after World War II.)[21] Saints in East Germany after World War II were cut off from the rest of the Church, including its temples. The members wanted to go to the temple in Switzerland, but the communist government restricted travel. However, after getting so many requests for visas, the Ministry of Religious Affairs in Berlin finally told President Burkhardt, who was essentially the leader of the Church in the GDR (German Democratic Republic), "You have made it abundantly clear why it is important for your people to attend a temple, but what we do not understand is why your church does not build a temple right here."[22]

Shortly after, Church leaders made plans to build a temple in the GDR. It was an amazing blessing that matched promises that President Monson made to the German Saints years before when he said, "If you will remain true and faithful to the commandments of God, every blessing any member of the Church enjoys in any other country will be yours." The building and dedication of the Freiberg

---

20. David F. Boone and Richard O. Cowan, "The Freiberg Germany Temple: A Latter-day Miracle," in *Regional Studies in Latter-day Saint Church History: Europe*, ed. Donald Q. Cannon and Brent L. Top (Provo, UT: BYU Religious Studies Center, 2003), 147–67.

21. *Merriam-Webster.com Dictionary*, s.v. "iron curtain," accessed July 24, 2024, https://www.merriam-webster.com/dictionary/iron%20curtain.

22. Boone and Cowan, "The Freiberg Germany Temple."

Temple in 1985 under the Iron Curtain was an answer to prayers and part of the fulfillment of the Lord's promises to the Saints in Germany. (You can read more about the temple's history at the end of this book in the section titled "History of the Germany Berlin Mission and the Freiberg Temple").

I loved learning about the temple's history, and the Freiberg Temple's story added to its sacred spirit. The Freiberg Temple and chapel sit beside each other atop a hill. In the summertime, the lush, green lawn blooms with flowers. Streaming sunlight bathes the sacred buildings in a rich golden glow. It's a peaceful, beautiful place.

That summer, I was elated to be able to be a part of the open house. Freiberg was my first mission area and felt like a home away from home. Furthermore, all of us sisters were excited because we loved serving at the temple. It was amazing to feel the Holy Ghost so strongly and interact with people touched by the Spirit there.

One pleasant but sweltering afternoon at the week-long open house, I was stationed in a large white tent with two other sisters to help outside the temple. The tent stood adjacent to the temple, and volunteers had supplied it with cool fans, comfy chairs, and tables topped with copies of the Book of Mormon. In the tent, our job was to welcome visitors who had just received a temple tour and ask them if they had any questions. I loved it! It was amazing to see so many faces lit up with excitement. Members and nonmembers alike enjoyed the tour.

Having just learned about the gospel, one lady approached me, sharing how she was impressed by the temple tour. It was clear from the light in her eyes that the Spirit had touched her. After talking about the temple, she asked me about myself and my mission. I felt so comfortable that I let my Perfect Barbie Robot act slip, and I ended up gushing to her about loving Germany's culture. I said, "Yes, I've loved being in Germany! I've always loved fairy tales, and I've enjoyed seeing castles here! They're magical and amazing."

After my excited outburst about the castles, I worried I had gone too far with being myself. Had I annoyed or offended the lady?

Nope! The lady simply smiled and replied, "What castles have you seen?" She seemed to warm up to me more, and we continued to talk about Germany and mission life. I think the woman appreciated a foreigner admiring her country's culture. While I had many other conversations that day, I have never forgotten the connection I felt with that woman. I hope she remembers her time in the temple that day and the Spirit she felt.

That conversation taught me an important truth that was as surprising as a slap in the face but as sweet and comforting as a warm hug: Being yourself *works* and is an effective missionary tool! People appreciate honesty and authenticity. By being your true self, you allow others permission to do the same, which fosters more genuine connections. It enables you to help others by accessing the talents the Lord has given you, which invites the Spirit into your interactions. Not only does being yourself work, but it also brings joy and confidence. There is no need to try to play the part of a Perfect Barbie Missionary Robot when God created you to be a Striving Unique Missionary.

Poison Envy

There was one sister I served with, Sister Bailey, who was an absolute beauty queen. Literally, she looked like a model or a Disney princess. I envied her long brunette tresses and craved to have a face half as pretty as hers. The transfer we served together[23] was a major crash course for me on the perils of envy and the importance of self-love and confidence. Let me explain what went down.

It was my second transfer in the area, and I loved the ward and its members.[24] My new companion, Sister Bailey, brought with her new ideas, and she wanted to do things differently. Sister Bailey was not only smart, spiritual, and gifted, but it was no secret that she was arguably the prettiest sister in the entire mission. On top of her beauty, she had a quick wit and a self-assurance that I found both intimidating and admirable. Using the worldly scales of beauty and self-assurance, I considered her to have greater credibility and authority than me, so I handed her the reins. I left all of the work and decision-making to her (which, I found out later, caused her a lot of stress). I wasn't using

---

23. A transfer refers to a period of six weeks within the mission field. After six weeks, missionaries may get called to serve in a new area and/or with a new companion.

24. A ward refers to a Latter-day Saint congregation.

my talents or being an effective missionary. I became immobilized, unable to take action. My influence dwindled as I focused my heart and mind on her strengths and my weaknesses. I envied her confidence, intelligence, social poise, and, most of all, her beauty. I was amazed when she told me stories about young men drooling over her. I wanted her stories to be my own. I wanted to be beautiful and be liked by boys too!

When we went finding (a term that means looking for people to teach by inviting all to learn about the gospel), all the men would stare at her, talk to her, and flirt with her. I became invisible to the male eye for six weeks while standing beside her. People would constantly compliment her beauty. I felt like a dumpy old hag and continued to waive my right to make decisions. I was miserable.

One Sunday at church, an observant sister noticed my pains by the downtrodden look on my face and through the help of the Spirit. She encouraged me, saying, "You can be confident with who you are, with your skills." I looked up to this sister and valued her opinion; however, I was too sad and too set in my jealousy to accept her advice.

I didn't realize it then, but my jealousy directly impacted my confidence. Envy was not just a sin but a poison. The more I focused on my companion and how I wished I was as pretty and talented as she was, the less worthwhile I felt as a person. As President Kimball taught, while service adds "substance" to our souls,[25] envy diminishes it. Being jealous of Sister Bailey diminished my sense of self.

Although I was living a self-inflicted curse at the time, I can now see that that transfer was a blessing in disguise. I hope to remember the lesson I learned: Don't let envy consume you! Sisters, join me in striving to value other people's opinions and be grateful for (not jealous of) their talents and abilities. Be confident in yourself by focusing on and discovering your talents. No matter our shape, size, abilities, possessions, or beauty, we are all princesses whose inheritance is an eternal crown. No one is a threat to your crown! Be confident in who you are, be willing to learn, appreciate other people's contributions, and you will flourish!

---

25. Spencer W. Kimball, *Teachings of Presidents of the Church: Spencer W. Kimball* (2011), 79.

YOMO Truths: Be Yourself

You may be wondering, how does being yourself help you YOMO? Well, sisters, being yourself is the only way to truly YOMO. Trust me. I spent so much time worrying about what other people thought of me, comparing myself to my beautiful and confident companions, and focusing on my flaws and feeling inadequate that I sometimes made myself miserable. I was prideful. President Ezra Taft Benson, in his talk "Beware of Pride," taught, "The proud depend upon the world to tell them whether they have value or not. Pride is ugly. It says, 'If you succeed, I am a failure.'" [26] I had fallen into the trap (and often still do) of thinking that the world and my achievements define my worth instead of remembering my divine worth in God's eyes.

As a competitive person, I struggle with wanting to be number one, to be liked by others, and to matter in the eyes of the world. However, a better path is remembering our true worth and not viewing life as a huge competition. The world wrongfully teaches us that to "win" in life, we must be the wealthiest, the most talented, and the most beautiful. In God's eyes, we all matter and have been given talents to share with others. "Winning" in life in a gospel sense is more about faith, love, reaching our potential, and helping others reach their potential. In the book of Ecclesiastes, the speaker, or "the Preacher" as he's called, compared the vanity of the world to the peace found in God and stated, "Let us hear the whole conclusion of the matter: Fear God and keep His commandments: for this is the whole duty of [humankind]" (Ecclesiastes 12:13). We don't need to be "better" than others; we just need to be our best selves and follow God.

How can we live by the gospel perspective when the world is so loud? How can we remember our worth and not feel inadequate when someone is smarter, richer, prettier, kinder, or more [fill in the blank] than us? President Benson said, "If we love God, do His will, and fear His judgment more than men's, we will have self-esteem."[27]

I love that quote! (Even though I must confess I don't live it perfectly.) The more we focus on God and do His will, the less we worry

---

26. Ezra Taft Benson, "Beware of Pride," *Ensign*, May 1989, 6.
27. Ezra Taft Benson, "Beware of Pride," 6.

about what others think of us. We can develop self-confidence, enabling us to be ourselves more fully as missionaries and as daughters of God. Don't let worldly expectations or cultural molds of an "ideal woman" keep you down or hold you back. Be yourself. Know that you don't have to measure up to anyone else. Just do your best, and God will see your sincere efforts and bless and comfort you as you serve Him.

YOMO Tips on Being Yourself as a Missionary

1. **Build your worth based on what God thinks of you instead of what the world thinks of you.** This is definitely easier said than done. I have a strong testimony of the worth of souls yet still find myself slipping into worldly comparisons and labels. Here are a few strategies that help me remember my divine worth: I review quotes that resonate with me about the worth of souls. When I'm struggling, I pray for extra help. What especially helps me worry less about what the world thinks is remembering the gospel perspective and the ultimate sacrifice the Savior made for us all individually because He loves us. I encourage you to pray and ponder and discover ways to remember your true worth.

2. **Strive to compare yourself to others less.** I use the words *strive* and *less* instead of "stop comparing" because comparison is a natural human tendency and improvement is a lifelong process. So don't demand perfection of yourself, but whenever you catch yourself making a mental comparison, I challenge you to pause, take note, and replace your inner critic with a more positive thought. Your self-deprecating thoughts are not reality. Comparisons can make us feel prideful and above someone, but more often, I think we women compare ourselves to others and feel like we fall short. In his talk "Forget Me Not," President Uchtdorf said, "We spend so much time and energy comparing ourselves to others—usually comparing our weaknesses to their strengths. This drives us to create expectations for ourselves that are impossible to meet. As a result, we never celebrate our good efforts because they seem to

be less than what someone else does."[28] Sisters, don't compare your weaknesses to someone else's strengths! Comparisons are never fair, as President Uchtdorf pointed out. God bestowed *you* with specific gifts and knows that you have something amazing to contribute to His work, so serve and celebrate your progress!

3. **Understand that becoming Christlike means you can still be you:** As disciples of Christ, we all are asked to become more like Him throughout our lives. As missionaries, we literally wear His name on our clothing. However, becoming like Christ doesn't mean we can't be ourselves. It just means we need to strive to become our *best selves,* a more complete, divine version of ourselves with the Savior's help. So as you study chapter six of *Preach My Gospel* ("Seek Christlike Attributes") and strive to develop such attributes, remember that gaining greater faith, love, and hope doesn't mean you have to give up what makes you *you*. It just means putting in the spiritual effort and relying on the Lord to help you become more like Him.

4. **Utilize your talents.** One of the best ways to YOMO and to be yourself is to use your God-given talents. In a mission letter to me, my dad wrote, "Develop your talents as a missionary. Do this by taking time for yourself through personal study and prayer. You can develop the talents you have by understanding yourself and using your strengths as you serve a mission." Be creative! Reflect on what you love doing and what you're good at, and see if you can incorporate it into your missionary service. For example, my second trainer was a gifted artist. She drew vibrant pictures with chalk during our street displays,[29] and her art drew more people to hear about the gospel message. Another companion of mine was a talented violinist who used

---

28. Dieter F. Uchtdorf, "Forget Me Not," *Ensign* or *Liahona*, Nov. 2011, 120.
29. Street displays in my mission refer to how missionaries, sometimes accompanied by members in the area, would set up tables with Church materials on the street and try to talk to everyone who passed by.

her music to bring the Spirit into every room. I felt like my talents were less obvious, but I let my passion for a good story motivate me to talk to people and get to know them. Hearing people's stories inspired me, and I enjoyed getting to know the people I was called to serve. Your personality can be included as one of your talents. Be yourself, use your talents, and serve others in ways that resonate with you. For example, if you like castles, don't be afraid to talk about castles! Heavenly Father will send people along your path who you can uniquely bless just by being yourself and giving of yourself.

5. **Develop new talents and strengthen old ones.** In addition to using your talents, you can develop new talents to help you in your missionary work. In Matthew 25:13–17, Jesus gave the parable of the talents. In this story, a man gave his servants talents (or money). To one of his servants, he gave five talents, to another two talents, and to the last servant he gave one talent. The servants given multiple talents went and doubled what they had received, but the last servant was afraid and hid his talent (see Matthew 25:24–25). The lord rebuked the last servant, but he praised the other two for being good and faithful and made them rulers (Matthew 25:20–29). What does this parable teach us? Elder Ronald A. Rasband explained, "The Lord made it clear that it is not good enough for us simply to return to Him the talents He has given us. We are to improve upon and add to our talents. He has promised that if we multiply our talents we will receive eternal joy."[30] Heavenly Father has commanded us to increase our talents, and a mission is a great time for you to strengthen your existing talents and pursue new ones, with a spiritual focus. For example, you can dive into your study of the scriptures and increase your knowledge of gospel principles. Or you can hone your teaching skills by thinking of new and creative ways to share the missionary lessons with others. These are just two examples among millions of possibilities.

---

30. Ronald A. Rasband, "Parables of Jesus: The Parable of the Talents," *Ensign*, Aug. 2003.

6. **Pray for spiritual gifts.** These new talents could include spiritual gifts. President George Q. Cannon explained how these gifts work: "Every man and woman in the Church of Christ can have the gifts of the Spirit of God divided to them according to their faith and as God wills. . . . If any of us are imperfect, it is our duty to pray for the gift that will make us perfect. . . . God has promised to give the gifts that are necessary for [our] perfection."[31] President Cannon informed us that spiritual gifts are invaluable resources in our quest to become like Christ. He said that if we struggle with a particular sin, we can pray for the gift that will help us overcome it. We can use spiritual gifts to magnify our efforts and help us become more like Christ. *Preach My Gospel* teaches that "just as vital as what you do is *who you are* and *who you are becoming*."[32]

As missionaries, we can become our best selves as we ask for spiritual gifts and strive to become more Christlike. During my missionary service, I wish I had utilized spiritual gifts more often by learning more about them and fervently praying for them "with all the energy of [my] heart," as Moroni instructed us to do (Moroni 7:48). When I did pray for specific gifts, like greater charity, my heart was softened and I was able to love the people around me more. As you seek to be your full self—your best self—spiritual gifts will help you develop Christlike attributes and be more in tune with the Spirit. God wants to bless us and help us succeed. With His help, we can become more like Him and bless the lives of others as we utilize our talents and spiritual gifts.

YOMO Personal Strengths Activity

Read the following advice from my dad in a letter he wrote to me at the beginning of my mission. (My dad served in the Nevada Las Vegas Mission from 1985 to 1987 and always gave me great counsel about serving.)

---

31. George Q. Cannon, "Seeking Spiritual Gifts," *Ensign*, Apr. 2016, quoting *Latter-day Saints' Millennial Star*, Apr. 23, 1894, 258–61.
32. *Preach My Gospel: A Guide to Sharing the Gospel of Jesus Christ* (2023), 123; emphasis in original.

"Do not try to be like some ideal missionary that you have imagined in your head, like some type of fairytale missionary. Be yourself. The Lord has called you, not the imaginary missionary, to serve. The Spirit works through you as you utilize your personal strengths."

I love my dad's advice. His message is not to set unrealistic expectations for ourselves but to be ourselves as we serve, and that as we use our talents, the Spirit will help us reach people. Sisters, YOMO by being yourself and accessing your divine gifts!

Reflection Questions

1. Prayerfully ponder your personal strengths and talents. What are you good at? What do you enjoy? How do you like to help people and connect with them?

2. Write down your talents and strengths in a journal. Or discuss and share your talents with a parent, Church leader, or friend. You can ask them, "What are my talents?"

3. How can you use your talents to bless others now?

4. How can you use your talents as a missionary?

5. How can using your talents and praying for spiritual gifts draw you closer to the Savior?

Study Session: Divine Guidance on Being Yourself and Fighting Jealousy

- Mindy Raye Friedman, "Truth, Lies, and Your Self-Worth," *New Era*, Jan. 2014, 24–27.

- Ezra Taft Benson, "Beware of Pride," *Ensign*, May 1989, 4–7.

- Jeffrey R. Holland, "The Laborers in the Vineyard," *Ensign* or *Liahona*, May 2012, 31–33.

- Jeffrey R. Holland, "The Other Prodigal," *Ensign*, May 2002, 62–64.

- George Q. Cannon, "Seeking Spiritual Gifts," *Ensign*, Apr. 2016, quoting *Latter-day Saints' Millennial Star*, Apr. 23, 1894, 258–61.

- Gary E. Stevenson, "Promptings of the Spirit," *Liahona*, Nov. 2023, 42–45.

- Max Lucado, *You Are Special* (Wheaton, IL: Crossway Books, 1997).

- Gospel Topics, "Spiritual Gifts," Gospel Library.

- Matthew 25:14–30; Moroni 10:17–25; Doctrine and Covenants 46:27–33; Articles of Faith 1:7

3
DEALING WITH PERFECTIONISM

You don't have to be fully converted on day one.
Progress, not perfection, is the goal.

"And see that all these things are done in wisdom and order; for it is not requisite that a man should run faster than he has strength. And again, it is expedient that he should be diligent, that thereby he might win the prize; therefore, all things must be done in order." —Mosiah 4:27

PROGRESS, NOT PERFECTION

When I stepped into the Berlin airport on my first day in Germany as a missionary, I was surprised by how disoriented I felt. In fact, I felt as stiff as my new, unworn silver boots that my dad had sacrificed his online credit to buy for me. However, as the thrill of being in a new place caught up to me (a place I had always dreamed of visiting, thanks to my high school German teacher and the Grimm Brothers), I was eager to start what felt like a grand quest doing an important work.

Before my mission president and his wife sent me and the other new missionaries to our first areas, they drove us to a hill near the cities of Dresden and Meissen, where President Monson gave a dedicatory prayer for the mission. As Paul VanDenBerghe explained, on April 27, 1975, President Monson, then Elder Monson, "offered a prayer rededicating the land for the advancement of the gospel."[33]

On a grassy hill overlooking the town, we gathered in a grove of trees and read the dedicatory prayer together. As I heard the promises that God had made to the German people, I felt peace and excitement—a deep, reverent excitement for the work that is hard to put into words. Standing beneath the emerald leaves, I gazed at the city below with its maze of streets and houses, imagining all the shopkeepers and families and citizens being interested in the message. At that moment, the Spirit reconfirmed to me the importance of sharing the gospel and the special mantle of being a full-time missionary. There were people in Germany ready to hear about the gospel!

The next few days were a whirlwind of names, faces, and meetings with other brand-new missionaries, and then, before I knew it, I was dragging my suitcases across the gleaming cobble-stone streets of my first area, Freiberg. I still felt nervous, but I had been spiritually fed from the initial activities. I couldn't believe I was actually there, on the German streets, about to embark on an indescribable spiritual journey. I felt like a first-year witch at Hogwarts: overwhelmed by everything and intimidated by everyone, but so grateful to finally be where I was meant to be.

My first few weeks on the mission were simultaneously amazing and difficult. I loved my companion (my trainer), who was sincere and loving as she taught me how to be a missionary, and I enjoyed being immersed in a foreign culture and meeting new people in Germany. However, I struggled to adapt to the missionary lifestyle. I missed having alone time and doing things the way I wanted. In one of my emails to my family, I literally wrote, "I think obedience is an important topic for me to learn about right now because some of the rules seem a little dumb (like standing outside when your companion

---

33. Paul VanDenBerghe, "A Foundation of Strength in Germany," *Ensign*, Aug. 2000.

backs out [a car]), but I know it's not so much about the rules but more about my attitude." (Funny story about the car rule: One time, I wasn't paying attention when my trainer was backing our car down a ramp, and she almost hit another vehicle because of my poor signaling. #humbled.) I was right that it was about my attitude, but I had trouble improving it at first. I didn't understand all the rules and felt overwhelmed by the idea that my life was all about service now. I often asked myself, "Am I really willing to give up what I liked doing and focus on other people for a whole year and a half?" I wasn't sure I could do it.

At some point early on, my trainer gave me a few talks to read on how to become a converted and consecrated missionary. Conversion to the Lord is defined as "a change in our very nature" and a lifelong process of becoming more like Christ. [34] Consecration is when you "dedicate" something to "a sacred purpose," such as giving your talents, time, and resources to God.[35] Elder Neal A. Maxwell taught that "ultimate consecration is the yielding up of oneself to God."[36] So I learned that a converted, consecrated missionary is one who is becoming like Christ, serving out of love for Him, and striving to give God their heart and will.

My trainer was a kind and energetic sister, a converted missionary herself, so I know she wanted to share these talks with me so that I too could become the best missionary I could be. However, I read those talks with the wrong perspective. They mentioned giving your whole heart to the Lord and being perfectly dedicated to His work, but all I could think was "I'm still not sure I want to do this" and "The bedtime rule is unnecessary." (After a few late nights, I realized why I needed to follow the curfew.) Basically, I could see the gap between me and the fully converted missionary, and the chasm was as vast as the Cave of Wonders in *Aladdin*. Actually, it was probably wider, and I didn't have a cool magic carpet to fly me across.

However, instead of sharing my anxieties with God or my companion, I fed my insecurities and let them grow. I resented the fact

---

34. Topics and Questions, "Conversion," Gospel Library.
35. Topics and Questions, "Consecration," Gospel Library.
36. Neal A. Maxwell, "Consecrate Thy Performance," *Ensign*, May 2002, 36.

that not only was I supposed to serve dutifully, but I was supposed to serve with all of my heart and with love. I thought to myself, "God is asking too much of me! How will I ever be able to give God my whole soul and put all my heart into the work?" I was too imperfect for such a perfect standard, and I felt like I'd never measure up.

Looking back, I can see the mistake in my perspective. I felt such resentment and stress because I read those consecration talks and felt pressured to become a fully converted missionary right at that moment. I thought I had to change and become a new person overnight or else I was a failure. However, I didn't realize that conversion is a *process*. Change is a *process*. It's a process we can't do without Christ's help. My trainer was right in sharing those talks with me, but I misinterpreted them. I wanted to be perfect at the beginning of my mission (and I still wasn't perfect by the end of it).

This is something I wish other sisters knew that I didn't realize back then—that progress is more important than perfection. Yes, we need to improve and become more converted disciples of Christ, but it doesn't happen in the blink of an eye. It's something we continuously strive for with the Savior's help. In his talk "What Lack I Yet?" Elder Larry L. Lawrence said, "To Him, our direction is ever more important than our speed."[37] So don't feel pressured like I did to become perfect overnight. Follow my fabulous trainer's advice: "Remember to not run faster than you have strength" (see Mosiah 4:27). Seek the Lord's help, draw closer to Him day by day, and gradually become the converted missionary you want to be—the consecrated missionary who strives and wants to give her all to the Lord and His work.

A second thing I want you sisters to know: those talks on consecration were *right*. The happiest missionaries are those who are converted, serving with love. This means *striving* to give your all to the Lord and putting your heart into the work, even if you sometimes fall short of that goal. I was never perfect, but as I slowly transitioned from wishing to do my own thing to focusing more on serving others, opening my heart, and trusting God, I became happier. Be patient with yourself as you become a more consecrated missionary. Please know that it's possible and only possible with Christ's grace. As you

---

37. Larry R. Lawrence, "What Lack I Yet?," *Ensign*, Nov. 2015, 35.

pray, strive to serve sincerely, and ask the Lord for His strength and help, you will become the best missionary you can be. That is a wondrous truth.

YOMO Truths: Progress Versus Perfectionism

Now that we've discussed how you don't have to be perfect, but that striving to become a converted missionary brings joy (see Doctrine and Covenants 4:2), let's review some practical and spiritual tips. First, let's contrast perfectionism with spiritual progress, and then discuss how to combat perfectionism in our daily lives as missionaries.

What is Perfectionism?

First, let's talk about what perfectionism actually means. One definition of perfectionism is "the tendency to demand of others or of oneself an extremely high or even flawless level of performance, in excess of what is required by the situation."[38] Another dictionary describes it as "a disposition to regard anything short of perfection as unacceptable."[39] (I know I've been guilty of that—almost all the time!) While wanting to improve and be your best can be healthy, perfectionism can reach toxic levels when it negatively impacts your health and well-being.

A BBC article on this topic explains the difference between adaptive (or "healthy") perfectionism and maladaptive (or "unhealthy") perfectionism. Knowing the difference between the two can help those of us who struggle with perfectionism. The author explained that "healthy" perfectionism is "characterized by having high standards, motivation and discipline," while "unhealthy" perfectionism is "when your best never seems good enough and not meeting goals frustrates you."[40] (Of course, *I've* never had thoughts like that . . . just kidding.) Ruggeri emphasizes that a "critical inner voice" distinguishes perfectionism

---

38. *APA Dictionary of Psychology*, s.v. "perfectionism," accessed July 24, 2024, https://dictionary.apa.org/perfectionism.

39. *Merriam-Webster.com Dictionary*, s.v. "perfectionism," accessed July 24, 2024, https://www.merriam-webster.com/dictionary/perfectionism.

40. Amanda Ruggeri, "The Dangerous Downsides of Perfectionism," BBC Future, Feb. 20, 2018, https://www.bbc.com/future/article/20180219-toxic-perfectionism-is-on-the-rise.

from healthy striving or conscientiousness. It involves "marrying your identity with your achievements," avoiding mistakes at all costs, and believing that you are a failure when you make a mistake. Because learning from your mistakes helps you improve and eventually achieve your goals, perfectionism is "self-defeating." Ruggeri adds that perfectionists feel more guilt, shame, and anger and that perfectionism has been linked to depression, anxiety, and stress.[41]

Furthermore, perfectionism is on the rise. According to an online press release, a study of a large group of American, Canadian, and British college students showed that perfectionism among young adults greatly increased from 1989 to 2016.[42] What can we do then to combat this way of thinking? One counseling department recommends identifying negative thought patterns, being more realistic in how you view situations, setting strict time limits on your activities, learning how to deal with criticism, accepting that it's okay to make mistakes, and implementing healthy goal setting.[43] The main objective with each of these strategies is to go from a mindset of "I must be perfect and can't make mistakes" to learning, improving, and progressing.

Progress Versus Perfectionism in a Spiritual Sense

Looking at issues like perfectionism from both a clinical and a spiritual perspective is helpful. So what have Church leaders said about perfectionism? In his talk "Perfection Pending," President Nelson pointed out that many Saints feel stressed about the commandment in Matthew 5:48 to be "perfect, even as your Father in heaven is perfect." The prophet went on to explain that in that verse, *perfect* was translated from the Greek word *teleios*, meaning "complete," and from *telos*, meaning "end," so the command in Matthew 5:48 doesn't mean "freedom from error" but signifies "achieving a distant objective."

---

41. Ruggeri, "The Dangerous Downsides of Perfectionism."
42. American Psychological Association, "Perfectionism Among Young People Significantly Increased Since 1980s, Study Finds," Jan. 2, 2018, https://www.apa.org/news/press/releases/2018/01/perfectionism-young-people.
43. University of Michigan, "Coping With Perfectionism," Student Life: Counseling and Psychological Services, accessed Feb. 1, 2023, https://caps.umich.edu/content/coping-perfectionism.

Heavenly Father does not expect us to be perfect today, but He asks us to follow Christ and strive to be obedient. President Nelson ended his address with this comforting quote: "Perfection is pending."[44]

I love that! How comforting is it that our prophet has told us we don't have to be perfect in this exact moment or even during this lifetime? Sisters, remember that you don't have to be perfect! You don't have to progress alone. You can rely on Christ and His grace. Elder Jeffrey R. Holland offered the comforting counsel that "the Lord blesses those who want to improve" and who "seek" to keep the commandments.[45]

So, sisters, never give up! Know you don't have to be perfect. Multiple Church leaders have assured us that we don't have to be perfect; we just need to keep trying. We need faith in Him who can help us eventually become perfect. I hope you will be less worried about being perfect, less hard on yourselves when you make mistakes, and more able to celebrate your victories than I was. If you learn this a little earlier than I did, your mission experience will be so much easier and more joyful. You'll be able to YOMO more!

YOMO Tips on How to Deal with Perfectionism on the Mission

1. **Set healthy goals.** As a missionary, you set goals regularly, from daily and weekly goals with your companion to personal ones. Strive to make achievable goals instead of perfectionist ones. One example of healthy goal-setting that my mission president taught us (and you may have heard about before) was "SMART" goals, an acronym first coined by George T. Doran[46] that means making plans that are Specific, Measurable, Achievable, Realistic, and Timely.[47] This method

---

44. Russell M. Nelson, "Perfection Pending," *Ensign,* Nov. 1995, 88.
45. Jeffrey R. Holland, "Tomorrow the Lord Will Do Wonders among You," *Ensign,* May 2016, 126.
46. Duncan Haughey, "A Brief History of SMART Goals," ProjectSmart, Dec. 13, 2014, https://www.projectsmart.co.uk/smart-goals/brief-history-of-smart-goals.php.
47. "Coping with Perfectionism."

can help you improve without experiencing burnout. On my mission, SMART goals helped me progress and stay positive. For example, I felt prompted to converse with more people on trains, street cars, and buses, but I was scared and didn't know if I could do it. So I set SMART goals about talking to X number of people per day on public transportation until I gradually became comfortable enough to approach people naturally when traveling.

2. **Change your perspective on mistakes and failure.** Okay, so this point is way easier said than done, but change your thinking about mistakes—that they're the *worst thing ever!*—to accepting them as *a natural part of your learning process*. My husband is always telling me that failures are the steps to success. As a perfectionist, this reminder is an annoying truth to hear. However, I know we will succeed as we give ourselves grace, allow ourselves to make mistakes and fail, and then strive to learn from those setbacks.

3. **Remember Christ.** My mission president once told me that if we feel like we have to be perfect, we're forgetting the role of the Savior. Because Christ atoned for our sins and died for us, we don't have to be perfect. Instead of demanding perfection of ourselves, we can continuously repent and strive to "come unto Christ and be perfected in him" (Moroni 10:32). Jesus Christ offers us unlimited second chances.

4. **Be true to your principles and goals.** Perfectionism grows in intensity when I try extra hard to meet other people's expectations and am more concerned with pleasing others than pleasing God. What helped ground and comfort me (and reduced my pride) was striving to be the kind of missionary I *personally* wanted to be and do things for myself and the Lord. As I tried to live according to my standards and focus less on other people's opinions, I felt peace and joy as I served. When I made mistakes, I would pray to God, and He would reassure me that He saw and accepted my efforts despite my

failures, helping ease the sting when I didn't meet my high expectations.

5. **Remember that repentance is a lifelong process**. Strive to repent and improve daily, and remember that God doesn't expect perfection but commends effort. Near the end of my mission, I wrote, "Repentance *is* the plan—it's not Plan B. It's about changing and becoming more like Christ. Daily repentance, taking inventory of your day with God, and listening to the Spirit does bring confidence and joy. Repentance is not always easy, but it works. And the love of Christ and hope of forgiveness can see us through." (This is part of a letter I wrote to myself at the end of my mission, following my mission president's instructions. The mission president sent us our letters two years after we came home. I quote this letter, my "finisher's letter," throughout my book because it contains useful spiritual principles and insights I learned in Germany.) Repent daily and celebrate your progress, sisters!

YOMO Activity: Give Yourself Grace

Are you ever tough on yourself in one (or maybe multiple) areas of your life? I challenge you to give yourself grace. Complete one of the activities below, and either write in your journal or talk to a friend or parent about what you learn.

Option 1: Try something new! Learn a new skill or participate in a new activity. Try something you're afraid to do because you're scared of failing. Make yourself a deal: "I get points for trying it out, even if I fail." Then have fun doing the skill or activity, and reward yourself for trying, no matter what the results are. You've got this!

Option 2: Set a SMART goal this week. The goal can be spiritual, educational, career-related, or so on. Evaluate your progress at the end of the week. If you have fallen short of your goal, practice applying grace. Note what you did well and make a plan on what you can improve next time. Whether you succeed or not, focus on the progress you made and the grace that Jesus Christ offers you. You don't have to be perfect!

Study Session: Perfectionism Versus Progression

- Russell M. Nelson, "Perfection Pending," *Ensign*, May 1995, 86–88.

- Jeffrey R. Holland, "Be Ye Therefore Perfect—Eventually," *Ensign* or *Liahona*, Nov. 2017, 40–42.

- Jeffrey R. Holland, "Tomorrow the Lord Will Do Wonders among You," *Ensign* or *Liahona*, May 2016, 124–27.

- David A. Bednar, "Ye Must Be Born Again," *Ensign* or *Liahona*, May 2007, 19–22.

- Regarding depression and perfectionism, see Jane Clayson Johnson, "Chapter 4: Toxic Perfectionism," in *Silent Souls Weeping* (Salt Lake City, UT: Deseret Book, 2018), 52–74.

- Moroni 10:32; 3 Nephi 9:13–14; Hebrews 12:22–23; Doctrine and Covenants 67:13

4

Joy

Flashy Ferraris and Prada purses don't bring joy,
but living the gospel of Christ does.

"And now, if we do not receive anything for our labors in the church, what doth it profit us to labor in the church save it were to declare the truth, that we may have rejoicings in the joy of our brethren?" —Alma 30:34

The Joy of Living the Gospel of Christ

Have you ever fantasized about driving a flashy sports car down a winding canyon on some trail near the ocean? It's a bright and sunny day, the wind is soaring past your designer sunglasses and perfectly flowing hair, and you're feeling alive and relishing the moment. Or have you ever dreamed of strutting down a red carpet in an elegant and stunning ballgown with roars of approval and applause following your every footstep? I don't know—maybe only I have such outlandish fantasies! Sometimes I'm tempted to think things like flashy sports cars and gorgeous gowns will bring me joy. However, my mission taught me the truth about what really makes people happy—it's living the gospel of Jesus Christ. Many members taught me this truth, but one particular sister's faith-filled example stands out to me.

I met this special sister, Schwester Kühn, in the middle of my mission. She lived in a house with gorgeous flowers blooming near its walls. Whenever we visited her, she would welcome us with a kind smile and something delicious to eat. (Her meals were so, *so* good. I can't even adequately describe them. For Christmas, she made this white-frosted marzipan cake, and it seriously looked and tasted like a fairytale!) Schwester Kühn was also a gifted writer and always had words of wisdom to share with us. Despite the cold German winter, she radiated warmth and kindness.

It wasn't just Schwester Kühn's food or words that impressed me. Her dedication to the Lord left a mark on me. She had faced some difficult challenges and circumstances in life, as many people do. However, she wore her trials with grace because she turned to the Lord and experienced *His* grace. Her commitment to the gospel of Christ was evident in how she sacrificed time to attend the temple weekly and how she ministered to her family, friends, and us missionaries. For example, when my companion needed to go to the doctor, and we knew we would need help understanding medical terms in German, Schwester Kühn volunteered to accompany us and translate for us. She also brightened my life with kindness and encouragement every time she saw me. She shared how the Lord was there for her and supported her in her challenges. I view her as a woman of strength because she focused her life on Christ.

What also impressed me about Schwester Kühn was her joyful glow. She was one of the happiest individuals I met on my mission. She radiated light and goodness and seemed to savor life. Her humor and love lit up the room. Her secret to happiness (which she was willing to share) was that she lived the gospel of Christ fully. While Schwester Kühn still had challenges, she experienced joy as she turned to the Lord during trials, sincerely served others, and received strength from attending the temple. Ultimately, Schwester Kühn taught me that true happiness does not come from external circumstances but from one's relationship with God.

Every week for eighteen months, I met many faithful members like Schwester Kühn—members who offered countless examples of how the happiest people dedicate themselves to living the gospel of Jesus Christ in every aspect of their lives. These individuals weren't perfect, but they were willing to make sacrifices for the gospel of Christ. Through their example, I received proof of President Nelson's words: "Here is the grand truth: while the world insists that power, possessions, popularity, and pleasures of the flesh bring happiness, they do not! They cannot! What they do produce is nothing but a hollow substitute for 'the blessed and happy state of those [who] keep the commandments of God.'"[48] I'm so grateful that I got to witness the faithful examples of the Church members in Germany. I have learned that knowing our divine identity and purpose in life, feeling peace when we fall short, receiving comfort in trials, and having a close relationship with God (which can strengthen our other relationships) are specific ways that following the covenant path brings joy. For eighteen months, I got to see what the true key to happiness is: following Christ.

The Joy of Charity and Relationships

It sounds a little cliché—the idea that "all you need is love."[49] I think the Beatles may have meant it a little differently, but still, it's true: all you really need *is* love. Only it's more than just love—it's charity, or "the pure love of Christ."[50] Jesus shared unconditional love with everyone He met, saw people's needs, and helped people feel seen. His focus was always outward, never self-serving, always genuine and deep. During my mission, I was blessed to meet many members and nonmembers who embodied aspects of this Christlike love. I had the opportunity to develop a small measure of charity myself (but I'm not going to lie—I still have a long way to go with that). I remember that some of the happiest moments of my mission revolved around the charity and love I felt from ward members during the holiday season in the Erzgebirge region (a mountainous area in the state of Sachsen).

---

48. Russell M. Nelson, "Overcome the World and Find Rest," *Liahona*, Nov. 2022, 97.
49. The Beatles, "All You Need is Love," track 11 of *Magical Mystery Tour*, Parlophone, 1967, compact disc.
50. Topics and Questions, "Charity," Gospel Library.

It was December, and Christmas was approaching. Being far from home for the first time during Christmas, I expected to feel a little sad. But I didn't—because of the charity that the ward members in Sachsen showed us missionaries that holiday season. I opened our apartment door early in December to find treats delivered from the ward! They surprised us with gifts and sweets the entire month of December. It was the best. Just imagine biting into a smooth and rich European chocolate or munching on a pleasurable, perfectly spiced Christmas cookie. Obviously, I was in love with the chocolate and the treats they gave us, but my companion and I also felt the Christlike love the members were sending us. They demonstrated charity to us by giving their time every day to help us feel seen, loved, and included.

The elders, my companion, and I were blessed to go to a Christmas market in the Erzgebirge region with a kind man from the ward, Bruder Meyer. To help paint the picture a bit, Christmas in Germany is a *big deal*. While I haven't had the opportunity to travel to other countries during the holidays, I'm pretty sure that Germany does Christmas the best. It's practically a month-long celebration there, with Christmas markets open in every city for each week of December. These Christmas markets were magical to experience. An entire town square would be filled with rows of booths that looked like miniature houses, sometimes blanketed in snow, and always lit up with festive lights. People sold splendid wooden candles and other hand-crafted items, as well as what really grabbed my attention: scrumptious donuts called Quarkbällchen, roasted almonds, and several beautiful meat and cheese-filled delights.

This particular Christmas market we went to with Bruder Meyer was special because the Erzegebirge region is especially known for its enduring Christmas traditions in its former mining villages, from its handmade wooden toys to its bright lights.[51] On those snowy streets in a picturesque Erzgebirge village, Bruder Meyer gave us a tour of the market, explaining traditions and pointing out items such as ornate nutcrackers and gingerbread cookies. My eyes darted from one booth to another, trying not to miss out on a single detail, and I felt warm

---

51. See "The Erzgebirge-Christmas Traditions," DW, Dec. 27, 2012, https://www.dw.com/en/the-erzgebirge-christmas-traditions/a-16462196.

inside despite the cold air seeping into my gloved hands and hitting my red cheeks. I was blessed to be experiencing the market with such a sincere and kind tour guide!

An hour or so later, Bruder Meyer said it was about time to leave. Before we left, I knew exactly what I wanted to get: a gingerbread heart. I desperately wanted one ever since I had learned about those treats in my high school German class, and I yearned to send one home. These hearts also had holiday greetings written on them in icing, and I thought they were beautiful.

Snow was lightly falling and we were headed to the car when I tentatively told Bruder Meyer, "Is it okay if we stop for a second? I really want to buy a gingerbread heart."

Bruder Meyer hesitated. He gave me a confused look, and I realized he didn't understand why I wanted a gingerbread heart so badly. So I explained how special it was to be seeing them now after learning about them in school.

Bruder Meyer's eyes lit up in understanding, and even though we were likely running late, he told the group to wait as I procured my gingerbread heart. Bruder Meyer showed me Christlike love by valuing my feelings and perspective, seeing and validating my needs, and constantly treating us missionaries with warmth, patience, and respect.

The Christmas season continued with joy. Not only do Germans eat delicious foods and plan fun festivities, but they also are very family-focused at Christmas, with three days devoted to celebrating Christ's birth. On Christmas Eve, Christmas Day, and the day after Christmas, three different members invited my companion and me to their homes, where we felt the joy of the season and the love of Christ. In fact, the light and warmth of Christmas made up for the cold and snowy German winter. One of the generous members who invited us into their home was Bruder Meyer, and it was in his home I realized another truth about joy.

On Christmas Eve, my companion and I spent a very cheery evening with Bruder Meyer and his wife and daughter in their home in Sachsen. The instant my companion and I stepped into their warm house, Bruder and Schwester Meyer showered us with love. I felt so welcomed by them! Bruder Meyer, as usual, was quite the hoot. (He would constantly crack jokes, and one time he held up a plastic bag toward me that was full of cow tongue, jokingly threatening to make me eat it.) Schwester Meyers was always kind and thoughtful. She showed the missionaries her love by knitting the cutest creations (like a panda bear that I got before leaving the area).

My companion and I enjoyed eating delicious raclette with them. Raclette is a Swiss dish that essentially involves heating cheese, scraping it from the heater, and eating it over your food.[52] We sat at their kitchen table, talking and laughing, roasting our cheesy dinners and getting seconds, then thirds, then fourths. After stuffing ourselves with tasty food, we retired to their living room with its comfy couches, a crackling fireplace, and a gigantic Christmas tree carved in wood and alit with candles. We turned off all the lights and watched the candle lights glimmer. It was magical. Bruder Meyer also entertained us with a tale from an old Erzgebirge-region storybook. He had a way of making the culture come alive. As he and his wife talked and joked with us, they made us feel like their own daughters. That memory of sitting on their couch and connecting with the Meyers, who welcomed us into their home during the holidays, is emblazoned in my mind forever. I felt at home, at peace, and intensely happy. It was the moment I experienced true charity, when I learned that happiness comes from connecting with people and giving and receiving genuine, outward-focused Christlike love. It was a magical revelation for me that could change my life if I let it—that if you focus on people and cultivate charity, you will find great treasures of happiness!

The Joy of Missionary Work

With her lioness courage and loving heart, Katarina was a faithful young woman I was blessed to meet. My companion and I met her after two elders from another city contacted her on the street. Since she lived within our area boundaries, we got to go meet and teach her. She was wiser than her twenty-something years and impressed me with her spiritual perspective.

---

52. See "What is Raclette?," Emmi USA, accessed Feb. 20, 2023, https://www.emmiusa.com/what-is-raclette/.

During our first visit, my companion and I taught Katarina about the Restoration and the Book of Mormon. She was interested and wanted to learn more. We invited her to come to church with us, and a couple of weeks later, she came! I was elated because coming to sacrament meeting for the first time is a big step. The following week, my companion and I knocked on her upper-level apartment, and she warmly welcomed us in. I was beyond excited to teach a friend of the Church[53] who was beginning to make spiritual commitments. We sat down in her living room and began to teach her. In my tender mercies journal, one of my mission journals in which I recorded daily blessings, I wrote the following:

> Our Termin (appointment) with Katarina! We taught the plan of salvation, and it's probably my favorite lesson I've helped teach so far. I tried to speak from the heart, we all felt the Spirit, and it was a special missionary moment for me. Katarina cried and said she already knows everything we told her. [She's always felt that there's more to life than this mortal journey.] She's felt like she wants to go back home but doesn't know where that is, but now she knows—heaven! With God. She said she's always asked, "Warum bin ich hier? (Why am I here?) Woher komme ich? (Where do I come from?) Wohin gehe ich? (Where am I going?)," and it was so cool that we got to teach her about the plan of salvation, something she really needed. I felt the Spirit, and I know God's love for her is great."

As we left, I noticed that Katarina looked happier than before the lesson. I left with the thought "I really loved teaching her that lesson." It was the neatest experience to testify of God's plan for us and to hear Katarina say that she felt like she had heard it before. She actually *had* heard it before—in the premortal council before this life! (see Abraham 3:24–28). As my companion and I continued to teach Katarina, I was always touched by her spiritual sensitivity. She possessed great faith and had a conviction in her heart that the gospel of Christ is real, that God has a plan for us, that the Savior can cleanse

---

53. "Friend of the Church" is a phrase that refers to an individual who is receiving lessons from the missionaries. This term has recently replaced the word *investigator*.

and heal us from sin, and that we can live again with our heavenly parents and our families in the eternities.

During my next transfer, Katarina decided to get baptized. It was a very spiritual experience. Bonding with Katarina, sharing my testimony, and teaching her brought me so much joy. One of my favorite missionary verses is Doctrine and Covenants 18:15–16, in which the Lord promises great joy to each of us as we serve Him: "And if it so be that you should labor all your days in crying repentance unto this people, and bring, save it be one soul unto me, how great shall be your joy with him in the kingdom of my Father! And now, if your joy will be great with one soul that you have brought unto me into the kingdom of my Father, how great will be your joy if you should bring many souls unto me!"

This is His work, and it's a work of joy. I never felt so happy as a missionary as when I was teaching and testifying of the gospel of Christ. It's our number one purpose as missionaries. As you invite others to Christ and share spiritual truths that are close to your heart, you will feel God's love for others and for yourself. Even when people choose not to commit to the covenant path, you can still feel peace. As you serve and pray, the Spirit will confirm to you that your work is good and that your efforts, even if imperfect, are accepted by God.

YOMO Truths: Joy

Sisters, I want your missions to be *joyful*. I want you to feel the joy promised to those who share divine truths with God's children (see Mosiah 27:27; Alma 29:9). I want you to feel happiness as you serve others with Christlike love and build relationships with them (see John 21:15–17; Mosiah 2:17). I also want you to feel the gladness that comes from being "all in" with living the gospel of Christ (see Alma 19:6, 13–14; Alma 26:11–12). So how can you experience this joy?

First, it's important to recognize the difference between joy and happiness. Elder David A. Bednar explained that joy is a "condition of great happiness that results from righteous living" and is not a temporary feeling but is "a spiritual gift and a state of being and becoming." On the other hand, the world's understanding of happiness is often centered around fun, which is temporary and involves entertainment or play.[54] Joy can be a constant in our lives, but we can't always feel happy. However, Heavenly Father wants us to experience happiness as well as joy. (This chapter focuses on joy, and the next focuses on happiness and fun.)

The Joy of Living the Gospel of Christ

For eighteen months, the example of faithful Church members in Germany taught me that striving to follow the covenant path brings happiness. That looks like turning to the Lord in times of trial, accepting His will, serving wholeheartedly in your calling, and developing a close relationship with the Savior. Each of us can also experience the joy that comes from living the gospel. Although everything in our lives won't go perfectly, we can always have joy in Christ, as President Nelson explained in his talk "Joy and Spiritual Survival": "My dear brothers and sisters, the joy we feel has little to do with the circumstances of our lives and everything to do with the focus of our lives. When the focus of our lives is on God's plan of salvation . . . and Jesus Christ and His gospel, we can feel joy regardless of what is happening—or not happening—in our lives. Joy comes from and because of Him. . . . Jesus Christ is joy!"[55]

The promise of Christ's gospel is the promise of joy. As we learn to rely on Christ more, we can have more joy despite setbacks, disappointments, and challenges. The question is, then, how can we receive this joy? President Nelson's answer is to follow the counsel found in Doctrine and Covenants 6:36: "Look unto [the Savior] in every thought." The prophet promises us that gratitude, obedience, and focusing our thoughts on Christ will help us experience more joy. We can pray to feel this joy, as President Nelson said, and joy will come to us as "our Savior becomes more and more real to us."[56]

I love that quote! The more we strengthen our relationship with the Savior, the more joy we feel. We can learn more about the Lord

---

54. David A. Bednar, in Marianne Holman Prescott, "Fun vs. Joy: Elder Bednar Says Joy Is Enduring and Eternal," *Church News*, Dec. 10, 2018.
55. Russell M. Nelson, "Joy and Spiritual Survival," *Ensign* or *Liahona*, Nov. 2016, 82.
56. Russell M. Nelson, "Joy and Spiritual Survival," 82.

and turn to Him more. I know that I have a lot of room for improvement in this area! On Sunday, I try to focus more on Christ by learning about His gospel and seeking His Spirit, and as a result, I feel a lot more peace and joy. During the week, however, I easily get caught up in my routines and focus less on Christ. When I add more spirituality to my weekdays, I feel more joy, not just on Sunday but every day.

I challenge you to put President Nelson's promise to the test. Strive to remember the Savior and His love for you and experience more joy. I know that whenever I remember Christ's love for each of us, I feel greater peace and hope and can better counteract the world's lies about my worth and purpose here on earth.

Finally, remember that your mission and message are all about joy. President Nelson said, "That is why our missionaries leave their homes to preach His gospel. Their goal is not to increase the number of Church members. Rather, our missionaries teach and baptize to bring joy to the people of the world!"[57] You can YOMO more easily as you remember that your whole purpose as a missionary is centered on joy.

Knowing that the purpose of missionary work is centered on joy, I invite you to reflect on how the gospel of Christ has brought you joy and how you can share that hope and knowledge with others. I encourage you to think of ways to increase the amount of joy you experience. Here are a few ideas to get you started or ways to find joy:

- Perform a random act of kindness for someone without expecting anything in return.

- When facing something difficult, remember the Savior is there for you, and imagine what He would do if He were physically here.

- Spend a couple of hours a week doing a positive activity that makes you feel happy and fulfilled, even if it isn't technically "productive" or helping you get ahead with school or a career.

- Take time to study the scriptures and words of the prophets this week.

---

57. Russell M. Nelson, "Joy and Spiritual Survival," 82.

- Pray to feel divine love, or listen to a song or watch a video about the Savior's love for you.

- Give yourself "screen-free time" daily or once a week, taking a break from your phone and social media.

- Go out to lunch with a close friend, or call a friend you haven't talked to in a while.

- Let go of a grudge or forgive someone.

- Spend time developing a talent.

- Implement a new positive habit to live a healthier lifestyle.

The Joy of Charity and Relationships

One of the greatest sources of joy on my mission was receiving and giving Christlike love. The faithful saints in Germany, the kind people we taught, and even random strangers made me feel loved. I learned the life-changing truth that love makes us happiest: God's love, and charity toward others. President James E. Faust explained this further, saying, "The golden pathway to happiness is the selfless giving of love—the kind of love that has concern and interest and some measure of charity for every living soul. Love is the direct route to the happiness that would enrich and bless our lives and the lives of others."[58]

As a missionary, I was happiest when I strove to serve others. Although I fell short and still fall short of President Faust's selfless definition of love, I have learned from the examples of those who reach out selflessly. In particular, the Christlike love the members showed my companions and me deeply touched my heart. By joining us in missionary work, welcoming us into their homes, making us feel like part of their families, and sharing their culture with us, they taught me that charity is what brings happiness, not being the prettiest or smartest or being "better" than others. I learned that although I obsess over and adore castles, no architectural wonder could fill me

---

58. James E. Faust, "Our Search for Happiness" (Brigham Young University devotional, Sept. 14, 1999), 5, speeches.byu.edu

with as much contentment and joy as connecting with people in an atmosphere of Christlike love.

So the next question is, how can we develop charity? Despite the great examples I was blessed with on my mission, developing charity myself was challenging. Too often, I was stuck in my own head, worried about what others thought of me or preoccupied with my wants and weaknesses. However, when I decided to trust God and open my heart to people by listening to them, caring about them, and serving them, I felt happy, confident, and fulfilled.

Sisters, we can all develop charity by praying for it and striving to act with love. Moroni 7:48 teaches us, "Pray unto the Father with all the energy of heart, that ye may be filled with this love, which he hath bestowed upon all who are true followers of his Son, Jesus Christ." Praying for charity gave room for the Spirit to soften my heart and helped me focus on others more. Additionally, we can develop charity by trying to reach out to the people around us, remembering their divine worth as sons and daughters of God. We can pray to see people through Heavenly Father's eyes (which is an important part of service, as Elder Renlund taught us in his talk "Through God's Eyes").[59]

Sometimes loving others isn't simple. Some people can seem harder to love, and for me, overcoming my selfishness, laziness, and jealousy was (and still is) challenging. But I know that as we pray and strive to see people through a divine lens, we will feel greater love for our brothers and sisters and will be able to serve them more authentically.

The Joy of Missionary Work

Missionary work is about joy (see Doctrine and Covenants 31:3), and nothing brought me more joy as a missionary than teaching people about the gospel of Christ and helping them progress on the covenant path. In Freiberg, I was blessed to see a family from China, the Zhang family, get baptized—a husband and wife and their daughter. It was

---

59. Dale G. Renlund, "Through God's Eyes," *Ensign* or *Liahona*, Nov. 2015, 93–94.

amazing to see this sweet family get baptized with proper priesthood authority[60] and take a necessary step towards salvation.

I also enjoyed getting to know the Zhang family and teaching the new-convert lessons to them. After enjoying an aromatic, sometimes spicy homecooked meal with them, my companion and I would sit at their kitchen table and teach them about gospel principles. Brother and Sister Zhang asked sincere questions, always seeking to expand their knowledge. They'd ask questions such as "How can we strengthen our faith in Christ? How do we know if God is pleased with our efforts?" We'd assure them that God sees their efforts and is pleased with their spiritual progress. They often expressed love and concern for their daughter as well, being loving parents. I became close friends with the Zhangs and felt Christlike love for them. Seeing them grow in the light of the gospel was a joyful experience.

While nothing was more fulfilling than sharing the gospel, sometimes my fellow missionaries and I felt we weren't getting to teach much. So I'd like to offer some tips on how you can feel joy even in times when you aren't teaching many lessons.

First, do what's within your control and let go of what you can't control. I was at peace when I knew I was giving it my best. Second, as you continue to search for people to teach, you can share uplifting messages with your companion and ward members. Third, you can always strive to share God's love with everyone you meet by offering a smile, a sincere compliment, or a helping hand. Sometimes such service may lead to someone's interest in learning more. Lastly, try not to get discouraged. Heavenly Father has prepared people to hear the gospel message, even in areas with smaller amounts of statistical success. Have faith, share God's love, and teach His gospel. You'll have opportunities to share your testimony, and you'll fulfill your purpose as a missionary and feel great joy.

---

60. The Church of Jesus Christ of Latter-day Saints is the only church with the priesthood, or "power and authority of God" given to man, to perform ordinances such as baptism. (An ordinance is a "sacred, formal act or ceremony performed by the authority of the priesthood" signifying that a covenant is being entered into or renewed). The Church claims apostolic authority directly from Christ and His apostles in the New Testament.

YOMO Activity: The Joy of Missionary Work

I love the missionary stories of the sons of Mosiah, particularly of Ammon defending the sheep and preaching to King Lamoni. I invite you to read or listen to the story of the sons of Mosiah, as found in the Book of Mormon (see Alma 17–27). Choose a couple of chapters that stand out to you. (Mosiah 27–28 shares their backstory—how they rebelled against the Church but then found their way back to God and later decided to preach to the Lamanites—while Alma 17–27 describes their missionary story, including their trials, faith, and success.) Learn about the joy these missionaries experienced and the joy you can feel as you share gospel truths. Choose one or two of the following themes to study.

1. **Joy in Christ**
   - Read Alma 19.
   - There are many descriptions of God's light in this chapter, particularly in verse 6.
     - What do you think "the light of the glory of God," the "marvelous light of his goodness," and "the light of everlasting life" mean?
     - Why did this light give King Lamoni such great joy?
   - Study verse 13 as well. Note the joy Ammon felt in verse 14.
   - If you have experienced the light and joy of Christ, write about it in your journal. Consider the following questions:
     - When have you felt God's light?
     - When have you felt joy in Christ?
   - If you're still seeking answers, learn more about the Savior and His Atonement. Study the scriptures and words of the prophets and apostles, and pray to know the truth for yourself. Ask your parents, Church leaders, and trusted adults to share their testimonies of Christ and the joy He offers us.

2. **The Joy of Being an Instrument in God's Hands**
   - Read Alma 26:1–3, 11–12, 26–27, 35–37.
   - In Alma 26, we read about the great joy Ammon experienced from being a missionary and an instrument in the Lord's hands. Ammon praised the Lord, saying, "I know that I am nothing; as to my strength I am weak; therefore I will not boast of myself, but I will boast of my God, for in his strength I can do all things" (Alma 26:2). Consider the following questions:
     - What can we learn from Ammon's example?
     - How can we "glory in the Lord" (verse 16) and experience joy as we serve Him?
   - In Alma 19:16–29, we read about a woman named Abish who was a convert. She went and told the people about what had happened to the king and queen, hoping those who listened would believe and experience the joy of Christ. However, when the people came together and gathered around the king, the queen, and Ammon, they argued about why the three had fallen (see verses 18–27). This was not the outcome Abish had hoped for (see verse 28).
     - What can we do when we hope for success but don't succeed?
     - Can we still experience the joy of missionary work when people reject us? Read Alma 31:38 as you ponder these questions.

3. **Joy in Others' Successes** (Disclaimer: This one is still a hard one for me, but Alma is an inspiring missionary in this regard.)
   - Read Alma 29:14–17.
   - Alma was happy about not only *his* missionary success but also about the success of his friends, Ammon and his brothers. Consider the following questions:
     - What can we do to be more like Alma?
     - How can we be proud of other people's achievements instead of feeling threatened by them?

- o Write in your journal or discuss with your friends how we can "not joy in our own success alone" (Alma 29:14) but experience a greater fulness of joy because of our fellow sisters' successes.

Study Session: The Joy of Living and Sharing the Gospel of Christ with Love

- Russell M. Nelson, "Joy and Spiritual Survival," *Ensign* or *Liahona*, Nov. 2016, 81–84.
- Cristina B. Franco, "Finding Joy in Sharing the Gospel," *Ensign* or *Liahona*, Nov. 2019, 83–86. (Start now!)
- Gary B. Sabin, "Hallmarks of Happiness," *Liahona*, Nov. 2023, 56–59.
- Scott Taylor, "Elder Soares: 5 Principles to Help Missionaries Find Joy — During Missions and After," *Church News*, July 1, 2019.
- "Chapter 1: Fulfill Your Missionary Purpose," *Preach My Gospel: A Guide to Sharing the Gospel of Jesus Christ* (2023), 1–16.
- The "Charity and Love" section of "Chapter 6: Seek Christlike Attributes," *Preach My Gospel: A Guide to Sharing the Gospel of Jesus Christ* (2023), 127.
- John 10:10–11; Doctrine and Covenants 31:3–5; Moroni 7:44–48; Alma 19:6, 12–14

5
HAVING FUN ON YOUR MISSION

You can have fun on your mission *and*
still be a successful and obedient missionary!

"Love and enjoy your mission. You should do things that make you happy. You are a missionary, but remember we are here on this earth to have joy. You can have great fun and joy as you serve. I worked hard but I also had fun."
—My father in one of his letters to me

YOMO Involves Having a Little Fun

Sometimes on my mission, I felt like having fun was a sin. Like if I enjoyed an activity or a meeting too much, I must be sinning and I needed to be more serious. I sometimes imagined that I should be more like a grim, medieval nun, eschewing all pleasure and grimacing through each day. Although I gratefully never lived up to these false expectations, I felt guilty about having fun until I eventually learned that finding enjoyment was okay. Going from grimacing to grinning was good for me *and* the work.

It was a warm summer evening in late June near the end of my mission. I was biking through an emerald-green forest in Köthen, a small town in east-central Germany, on an exchange[61] with Sister Campbell, who had gorgeous chestnut hair and bright brown eyes. The temperature was Goldilocks-perfect—not too hot, not too cold—and I was in rapture at the beauty of the thick summer foliage as we pedaled through rows and rows of sturdy trees. We were on our way to Sister Campbell's apartment where we would eat, rest, and then enjoy a full day of exchanges. Suddenly an ancient, regal-looking building appeared on our way home in this wonderland. There stood a stone structure, likely an old manor house, that to me looked like (you guessed it) a castle. Admiring the manor house was a magical moment for me. We didn't have to take the forest path home, but Sister Campbell thought I'd appreciate it, and she was always up for an adventure. It was one of the many things I liked about her, and to this day I remember how happy that bike ride made me.

The next day I was thrilled to wake up in a new city and was grateful to be with Sister Campbell because she was awesome! She was fun to be around, with her lively spirit and her energy and passion for the work. We started off our day biking through sixteen kilometers of rural beauty: sun-kissed cornstalks and lush green fields. I felt as free as the wind. Then we rode through a pleasant Dorf, or small town, and reached our destination: lunch with a member whose now-deceased husband had been a patriarch. She fed us physically and spiritually: physically with delicious crepes adorned with layers of Nutella and German applesauce that I still dream about, and spiritually with her testimony of trusting God. She said, "Trials will come, but pray to God and place your trust in Him, and He will help you and provide a way." I felt so happy and excited by this sister's enthusiasm and the Spirit I felt in her home.

In the afternoon, we hopped back on our bikes and went finding in a nearby village. Often, I struggled with finding, but not this

---

61. An exchange is when you serve with a different companion for a short period of time. "In a companion exchange, a young missionary leader . . . works with another missionary. During the exchange the leader will teach, train, and learn from the missionary." "Companion Exchanges," from chapter 2 of *Missionary Standards for Disciples of Jesus Christ*, ChurchofJesusChrist.org.

day. Sister Campbell was enthusiastic and friendly to all, so we had many great conversations with people in the village. It didn't hurt that the spiritual sister we had lunch with was the widow of a patriarch who had also been a beloved doctor. Everyone in the town knew him and loved him. When we approached people, they responded, "Yes, I know a Mormon," and we had great conversations with everyone on the street. (This is where I exclaimed to my family in my email, "Members really are the secret weapons of missionary work!" I probably should have used a more appropriate description, but you get the point.)

It was a super day. Sister Campbell's love for the work was contagious, and I had a lot of fun having neighborly conversations with people and even handing out a brochure about the plan of salvation. We even got an exclusive church tour from a priest. Later, when I was reunited with my original companion at the train station to return to our area, Erfurt, two former sister missionaries gave us ice cream. Basically, everything seemed perfect and beautiful and fun.

Not every day in the mission will feel like that though, so during the difficult days, hold on to positive memories and know that things will get better. You can find something to appreciate each day. As my dad told me, life is meant to be enjoyed, and missions are a part of your life. You're allowed to feel joy and have fun! Yes, fun should be kept within the parameters of the mission, but you *can* have fun as a missionary. That day in Köthen (and I had other days like it), Sister Campbell and I were obedient, and we had fun while doing missionary work. It's possible! Having fun helped me be a happier, healthier, and more committed missionary.

YOMO Truths: Having Fun

As a missionary who experienced more joy and success when I was having fun, I firmly believe that this is an important part of a YOMO mission. Of course, not every moment will be great, but you don't have to live like a medieval nun and eschew fun like it's evil. Respect your divine call to serve, but find moments and activities to enjoy. President Hinckley said, "And finally, in all of living have much of fun and laughter. Life is to be enjoyed, not just endured."[62] Follow a prophet's counsel and YOMO by finding joy in the journey.

YOMO Tips on How to Have Fun on Your Mission

1. Take advantage of preparation days! (One day a week, usually Monday, missionaries are given time to clean, buy groceries, do laundry, and do fun activities.) In line with your mission's rules, visit historical sites, museums, or famous landmarks. Not only is it a lot of fun but you can invite members to join you too, and you can connect with them as you learn more about their culture.

2. Enjoy the tender mercies and blessings that come your way. For example, in the first few weeks of my mission, my trainer and I had lunch with a kind family from the ward in Freiberg. And guess what? They had horses! So I got to pet one of the chestnut beauties. Being outside and doing something different rejuvenated my soul, and learning about their love for animals helped me connect with the family more.

3. Do something fun each day! (Within the mission rules, of course.) Be intentional about it. It doesn't have to be something big. My number one suggestion is to treat yourself to ice cream after a long day of finding! (You don't have to listen to me—in case you couldn't tell, I'm quite addicted to sugar. Just do something small to make you and your companion smile.)

4. Remember, you don't have to be a Perfect Barbie Missionary Robot to be a good missionary. You don't have to be a soldier either, doing everything in a uniform way. You can be creative with the work and find and teach in unique (Spirit-approved) ways. Elder Neil L. Andersen once shared about how young people in Boston spread the gospel message through blogging, and one member commented, "This isn't missionary work. This is missionary fun."[63] Feed your soul by making the work

---

62. Gordon B. Hinckley, "Stand True and Faithful," *Ensign*, May 1996, 94.
63. Neil L. Andersen, "It's a Miracle," *Ensign* or *Liahona*, May 2013, 79.

enjoyable. Having fun as you serve will not only help reduce stress and uplift your mood, but it will also put a light in your eyes that will make you even more approachable to people.

Here is one example of creatively serving: One of my companions and I made a poster called "Who is your hero?" The poster had pictures of superheroes with a large picture of Jesus in the middle. Our approach wasn't perfect, but it was fun to be creative and change our usual way of finding people. Let the Spirit guide you, and be creative! You can also make a game out of finding, such as turning to a random page in the Book of Mormon and incorporating that into your invitations to people or seeing who can find the most interesting person to talk to. The possibilities are endless!

5. My final tip: *Literally* make a plan to YOMO! During my second-to-last transfer, I did just that. My companion and I chose "YOMO" as our theme for the next several weeks. I wanted to inspire us to be bolder, braver, happier, and more confident missionaries. (As YOMO is the title of this book, you can see how hugely it affected me.) Without being too irreverent, I hope you will remember to YOMO and have a lot of joy and fun as you serve. As my companion wrote to me, "Wir mussen das Leben geniessen! [We must enjoy this life!] It's true! Life is great, we are children of a great and merciful God, and we are doing His work! We can always find a reason to find joy in life—that is literally why we are here."

YOMO Challenge: Have Fun this Week!

I challenge you to go out and do a fun activity! Choose something that gives you joy, either by taking time for yourself or by going out and doing something fun with your friends. Know that as a missionary, you can keep having fun!

Study Session: Having Fun as a Missionary

- 2 Nephi 2:25; Matthew 25:14–30; Doctrine and Covenants 123:17

6

Trusting Heavenly Father

I've never doubted God's plan for me! JK.
But it turns out that His plan is always greater than mine.

"And this is life eternal, that they might know thee the only true God, and Jesus Christ, whom thou hast sent." —John 17:3

The Lord Knows You Better than You Know Yourself

Sometimes the Lord pushes you to do things you're not comfortable doing. Mission life is like a crash course in overcoming your fears because you'll be asked to stretch yourself and reach new goals. It's a process of growth—of gradually learning to trust God more than you trust yourself.

Before my mission, I was convinced I knew what was best for me. (I guess I still often think that way. Okay, I *know* I still think that way. #stillneedtobehumbled.) I had a vision for my life. I knew what I was good at and awful at, yet the mission had a way of turning those things on its head. My strengths were still my strengths, but I learned to explore new areas and develop new skills. As for my weaknesses, they were made more apparent than ever before. (Learning about my weaknesses wasn't easy; however, it helped me rely on the Lord more.) During those eighteen months, I learned that the Lord knows me best and that I should listen to Him more often. He is the Supreme Being of the universe, and He knows all things, including the past, present, and future. As President Nelson said, "God knows all and sees all. In all of eternity, no one will ever know you or care about you more than He does."[64] These truths—Heavenly Father knowing us better than we know ourselves, and Him knowing what's best for us—are truths I'm still learning. I received an intensive crash course on those topics as a missionary. Let me tell you the story.

Finding . . . inviting individuals to learn more about the gospel . . . talking to strangers on the street . . . I hated it. I mean, I *wanted* to share the gospel message with everyone, and it was thrilling to meet new people, but often many of those encounters were awkward for me and resulted in rejection. I did not enjoy finding for the longest time, and as a previously shy person, it was a challenge for me throughout my mission. However, as I gave my best effort, I slowly started to enjoy finding more and more. It was a process!

About halfway through my mission, the Spirit kept prompting me to talk to more people on buses, street cars, and trains. Now, something you must know first: Germans typically do *not* like talking to strangers on public transportation—they prefer to be silent or talk quietly with travel companions. So sharing the gospel during a bus ride was super challenging and took lots of guts. In addition, we were not actually allowed to proselytize on public transportation, so we were expected to bring up small talk and hope that people would ask about our missionary name tags. Because I disliked both finding and small talk, I dreaded these instances. Also, I was usually exhausted from finding on the street, so I kind of saw traveling as a break from missionary work. (I know, not the right way to look at things!) However, I kept receiving promptings to try talking to more people on public transportation. One day, I finally started to listen, and I made a couple of attempts that week to talk to someone on the bus. It

---

64. Russell M. Nelson, "Choices for Eternity" (worldwide devotional for young adults, May 15, 2022), Gospel Library.

was really awkward at first. Some people would just stare at the window and completely ignore me. Others would listen but then not ask any questions. My usual approach was to compliment a lady's scarf or purse. Each week, I began to set SMART goals about talking to people on buses, street cars, or trains. Making a specific goal helped me be less anxious about the whole thing because once I reached my goal, I didn't make myself talk anymore.

Gradually, I noticed that I didn't mind talking to people on public transportation as much as I had thought. It felt more natural to compliment someone or ask a generic question instead of diving straight into the gospel message like my companions and I often did on the street. Occasionally, I even got a good conversation out of my humble attempts, such as questions about my life as a missionary.

Once, I even got to bear my testimony to a young woman on a train after a zone conference meeting in Hamburg, a city in northern Germany. My companion and I were sitting across from her on the upper level of a nice, efficient train, one of Europe's faster and fancier ones. My clever way of beginning the conversation was "Hello! I like your white sneakers." Thankfully, the young woman was kind and smiled at me. Spotting our black missionary tags, she curiously asked, "What do those name tags mean?"

I said, "We're missionaries for The Church of Jesus Christ of Latter-day Saints. We tell people about our faith."

The young woman said, "What do you tell people?"

My companion replied, "We talk to people about God's plan for all of us as His children. You are a child of God. Because He loves you, He sent you here on earth to learn and progress and one day return to Him."

I added, "Sometimes we make mistakes, but God sent His Son Jesus Christ to atone for our sins and die for us so that we can be forgiven and feel peace. After our earthly journeys, we can live with God again."

The young woman asked, "What's life like after death?"

I said, "We can live with our Heavenly Father again, and we can also be reunited with our families. It'll be a time of great joy."

The young woman listened and nodded attentively. As I shared my testimony with her, I felt a warm feeling in my heart. I felt the Spirit strongly, and I felt happy teaching her. I thought to myself, "Maybe the Spirit was right in prompting me to talk to people on trains after all." Before we got off the train, we handed the young woman a card with our contact information on it. Though we never saw her again, I hope she felt the Spirit and met with missionaries later on.

Until the last transfer of my mission, I was awkward and stiff on the streets, but I loved having conversations with people on public transportation. I had always viewed my social skills and disinterest in small talk as a weakness, and while I still was awkward at times (just ask my companions for the juicy details), this mode of finding became my favorite. Becoming more comfortable with talking to strangers took time. Whenever I relapsed and had an awkward encounter, I'd tell myself, "It isn't a big deal, I'll probably never see that person again," and I'd focus on what I could improve for the next time. The growth I experienced was worth the effort and fails it took to get there!

Throughout this process, I learned that God truly knows me and my strengths better than I do. For you, it may not be to start finding on buses, but when the Spirit directs you to focus on a certain activity, do it! The Lord wants to bless and help you. "Trust that He loves and knows you better than you love or know yourself. . . . Decide to have faith that His way will lead to guidance, opportunities, and joy like you never could have expected."[65]

Developing a Relationship with Heavenly Father

Sometimes on my mission, I felt overwhelmed, lonely, and consumed with what others thought of me. Through those experiences, I learned that God is truly on our side. As Romans 8:31 says, "If God be for us, who can be against us?" When I finally turned my heart over to God and accepted His will and help, I became a happier and more effective missionary. Let me share an example of when this happened.

A few months after being in the mission field, I couldn't sleep at night. It wasn't just because spring had melted into a sticky and hot summer and my apartment at the time had no AC. Whenever I would try to close my eyes and fall asleep, my mind was bombarded with worries. My thoughts would circle around the same concerns: "What

---

65. Gospel Living, "God Always Wins," ChurchofJesusChrist.org, Aug. 21, 2022.

does the ward mission leader think of me? What do the members think of me? What does the mission president think of me? I want to be a good missionary." I didn't realize it then, but I was caught in a whirlwind of pride. While it's great to want to be a good missionary, I wanted to be good for the wrong reasons. I yearned to impress people. I was more worried about *looking* like a good missionary than *being* a good missionary. I wanted the mission president, ward mission leader, and members to think I was great. Slowly I realized the stress I was putting myself under by caring so much about what other people thought of me, and I tried to focus more on what God thought of me and what I thought of me—to serve for God and for my dreams, not to impress others. It wasn't an easy or quick change, but focusing more on "Am I living up to my values and the potential God sees in me?" versus "Am I pleasing others and making them proud of me?" made me a lot happier, and I felt more peace.

During this time, I also felt like no one believed in me—that my mission leaders and fellow missionaries didn't really trust me or see me as a capable sister. (Whether or not this was true, I don't know. They were just my perceptions at the time.) But I learned that God still believed in me because He would send someone, a human angel, to pick me up whenever I fell. Or I would pray and feel Christ's love for me. It was beautiful to realize that no matter what people thought of me (or what I mistakenly believed that people thought about me), I had great worth in God's eyes. He believed in me as a missionary and knew I could serve and help others. This was a powerful truth for me.

Still, sometimes I had doubts about the work or the rules. I was frustrated that I wasn't perfect. Over a year into my mission, I realized I needed to stop being so stubborn and accept that I couldn't do this alone. I needed to fully open my heart to God, trust Him, and be willing to do things His way. I knelt in my apartment one morning after gradually coming to this realization, and I prayed to Heavenly Father. I asked for forgiveness regarding my mistakes, and I promised to strive to trust God, accept His will, and seek His divine guidance and aid.

One prayer doesn't necessarily magically change everything, but I committed to trusting God more fully and accepting His help from that moment on. I can't say I fully accepted His will, but I did my best to be obedient. I tried to follow the advice attributed to Saint

Augustine: "Pray like everything depends on God, then work like everything depends on you."[66] As I continued to open my heart to God and accept His divine help instead of thinking I could do things my way by myself, I was happier. I became a more effective and a more confident missionary. The changes were gradual, but they were constant from that day forward. Trusting God, opening my heart to Him, and accepting His help made all the difference for me. Specifically, that looked like accepting the mission rules and routines instead of following them halfheartedly, turning to God for help instead of stubbornly thinking I could handle challenges on my own, and increasing my desire to follow His will.

While the mission remained a roller coaster, with steep emotional highs and lows, I finally became the missionary I had always dreamed of being: converted, confident, and sincere. I fully embraced and enjoyed the mission with God's help. Never underestimate Heavenly Father's love for you. Even if other people doubt you, know that God never has and never will doubt you. There is always something you can give, something good you can achieve with His help. Just don't be as stubborn as me. Accept His help earlier on so you can YOMO more.

YOMO Truths: Trusting Heavenly Father

Sisters, from these stories I want you to remember three things. First, the Lord knows you better than you know yourself. Second, no matter what other people think of you, or what doubts you may have, the Lord *always* believes in you and your potential to do good. Third, trusting God and building a relationship with your Heavenly Father will help you become the best missionary you can be. Let's learn more about building a relationship with God.

Know that one of the most valuable things you can do on your mission is to draw closer to your Heavenly Father. John 17:3 reads, "And this is life eternal, that they might know thee the only true God, and Jesus Christ, whom thou hast sent." One of the primary purposes of life is learning about, loving, and trusting God and His Son. Your

---

66. Saint Augustine, "Saint Augustine Quotes," Brainy Quote, accessed July 25, 2024, https://www.brainyquote.com/quotes/saint_augustine_165165.

mission is the perfect time to develop that divine relationship further! Being close to God will help you in the work and will enable you to guide others to do the same.

To help us better understand what trusting God means, I'd like first to define the word *trust*. The *Merriam-Webster Dictionary* defines it as an "assured reliance on the character, ability, strength, or truth of someone or something" or "one in which confidence is placed."[67] Trusting in God means believing in His divine character and strength. It means knowing that you can safely rely on Him and His promises. I believe that to trust the Lord, we must first get to know Him. We can learn more about Heavenly Father and the Savior by studying the scriptures and talks given by Church leaders, gaining insights about their divine attributes. In addition, we can ask questions, listen to other people's testimonies, and pray to hear His voice.

Now, I have to be honest—developing trust in God was not (and still isn't) simple for me. I may or may not have a tendency to think I know best. (Okay . . . I struggle with that a lot!) But I know there is a lot of power in striving to open our hearts to God and trusting Him, believing that His promises apply to us personally. So the question is, How do we do that? What actual steps do we take to open our hearts to God and increase our trust in Him? Here are a few ideas.

Opening your heart up to God is an act of faith. The Bible Dictionary defines faith as "a principle of action and power."[68] Take the initial step of confiding in the Lord and praying more sincerely to Him about your doubts, fears, desires, and goals while believing that He is listening. Next, develop trust in God by living the gospel, keeping covenants, and following promptings from the Spirit. As a missionary, follow those promptings to talk to a stranger or to do something good that may seem random!

Another way you can build your relationship with Heavenly Father is by being humble (see Doctrine and Covenants 67:10; 112:10). For example, I had to admit that I couldn't YOMO on my own and that I needed the Lord's help. As my attitude changed and I learned to

---

67. *Merriam-Webster.com Dictionary*, s.v. "trust," accessed July 25, 2024, https://www.merriam-webster.com/dictionary/trust.
68. Bible Dictionary, "Faith."

rely more on God by admitting mistakes and weaknesses and turning to the Savior for strength, I was comforted as I prayed and was supported by the Spirit as I served. The Lord will do the same for you as you serve your mission! (See Ether 12:27.) Don't be afraid to give God your heart—meaning share your struggles and hopes with Heavenly Father—and allow the Spirit to change you to help you develop Christlike attributes and be more receptive to God's will. President Benson said, "Men and women who turn their lives over to God will discover that He can make a lot more out of their lives than they can."[69] He explained further that as we do His will, Heavenly Father will richly bless our lives, giving us more joy, peace, comfort, friends, and opportunities.[70]

Opening our hearts to God, trusting Him more, and doing His will leads us to a happier life. It means sincerely praying to Heavenly Father about our innermost concerns, acting on the Spirit's promptings to stretch ourselves and grow spiritually, and humbly accepting the Lord's way instead of our way. The blessings President Benson mentioned are available to all of us as we give our hearts and will to God. It's important to note that this is a lifelong process. I know you will feel joy and be successful as you open your heart to God and follow the promptings of the Spirit. In a letter to myself, I wrote, "The Spirit—the Lord—knows you better than you know yourself. He knows what you are capable of doing. He knows your fears and struggles. He knows it all—so trust Him and His plan." It all comes down to trusting your Heavenly Father and His promises.

Sisters, trust God and believe in His promises. Ultimately, everything He does for you and asks you to do is for your eternal benefit. Strengthen your relationship with Him, and you will have an amazing, rewarding YOMO experience.

---

69. Ezra Taft Benson, "The Great Commandment—Love the Lord," *Teachings of Presidents of the Church: Ezra Taft Benson* (2014), 42–43.
70. Ezra Taft Benson, "The Great Commandment—Love the Lord," 43.

YOMO Activity: Strengthen Your Relationship with God

Take time to say a heartfelt prayer to Heavenly Father. Pray about a personal concern you have, express gratitude for your blessings, or seek His guidance on a topic important to you. Start or continue a habit of personal prayer!

Study Session: Building a Relationship with Heavenly Father

- Kevin W. Pearson, "Are You Still Willing?," *Liahona*, Nov. 2022, 67–69.

- Dieter F. Uchtdorf, "Of Things That Matter Most," *Ensign* or *Liahona*, Nov. 2010, 19–22.

- Neill F. Marriott, "Yielding Our Hearts to God," *Ensign* or *Liahona*, Nov. 2015, 30–32.

- 1 Thessalonians 2:4–6, 19–20; John 17:3; Isaiah 55:8–9; Alma 36:3; 2 Nephi 22:2–5; Doctrine and Covenants 11:12

7
DIVINE HELP

Like a super squad, a trusty crew, or a heroic team,
angels will have your back. The Savior will too.

"And whoso receiveth you, there I will be also, for I will go before your face. I will be on your right hand and on your left, and my Spirit shall be in your hearts, and mine angels round about you, to bear you up." —Doctrine and Covenants 84:88

GOD WILL SEND ANGELS YOUR WAY

Sometimes life is hard. And missions are hard, too. However, as challenges come, the Lord will not leave you alone. He will send His Spirit to comfort and cheer you up. As Alma 7:12 teaches, Christ "will take upon him [our] infirmities, that his bowels may be filled with mercy . . . that he may know according to the flesh how to succor his people according to their infirmities." You can always turn to the Savior because He is the One who understands all things—who perfectly understands you.

In my mission, we had a special way of remembering to think of Christ and His love for us. It was called "The Glance." When I served in my first city, Freiberg, my zone leaders gave each missionary a goal: whenever we got rejected, instead of getting depressed and discouraged, we were to "glance" down at our missionary name tags and remember who we represented. In my email to my family that week, I wrote about this concept: "We are representatives of Jesus Christ, and that is amazing!" On your mission, when you face rejection or discouragement, glance down at your name tag and remember who you represent. The Savior is on your side and will walk with you each step of your mission. He will strengthen and comfort you.

Sometimes comfort from God comes in the form of angels. The Bible Dictionary defines angels as "messengers of the Lord."[71] I believe angels are real and that you can feel heavenly influence from ancestors beyond the veil. As Doctrine and Covenants 84:88 reads, "I will be on your right hand and on your left, and my Spirit shall be in your hearts, and mine angels round about you, to bear you up." I know that divine help is real and that most often, the angels God sends us are not from the other side of the veil but are ordinary human beings here on earth. Heavenly Father sends these wonderful people to comfort and console us, help us feel His love, and give us hope to take another step further on our journeys.

I'd like to share a story about one such angel. Near the middle of my mission, I was stressed and unhappy about my performance as a missionary. I felt like everything was too hard, too much was being asked of me, and I wasn't doing a good enough job. Amid this trying transfer, my companion and I did exchanges with two sisters staying in Freiberg, which meant we got to travel there. I have such a great love for the city with the temple and super kind members. It was comforting to be back. During the exchange, I got paired up with one of the sisters from my MTC group, Sister Fröhlich. An Austrian beauty, she was in her late twenties and radiated the pure love of Christ. She was deaf, and through the use of cochlear implants, she would share comforting pieces of wisdom with us sisters. I loved being with Sister Fröhlich and always felt the Spirit strongly whenever I was with her.

During this exchange, Sister Fröhlich and I had the opportunity to attend an endowment session at the Freiberg Temple. Going to the

---

71. Bible Dictionary, "Angels."

temple is always spiritually rejuvenating, but as a missionary, it felt especially refreshing. After our endowment session, Sister Fröhlich, with her radiant smile and flowing dress, shared something with me that was both a tender mercy and a testimony. Looking into my eyes with kindness, she said, "Sister Shoaf, the gospel of Christ gives us everything we could ever want. The temple blessings promise that we can be together forever with our families, that we can live with God again, and that our lives have purpose. What more could we want?"

Her faith-filled testimony left an impression on my heart, and her words lifted me from the distressed state I had been in. On my mission (and still today), I sometimes got caught up in things that don't matter—things related to pride, beauty, and popularity. But Sister Fröhlich taught me what really matters: the gospel. Because of the faith and love she radiated, she became one of my mission angels. Every time I saw her at a meeting, I felt comforted just by being in her presence. Her testimony—her reminder that the gospel of Christ is a message of hope, joy, and love—has stuck with me for years. We can have hope in life because of Christ and His gospel, and His earthly angels often remind us of His love. You will not be left comfortless on your mission, *or* on your life mission (see John 14:18). God will send the Holy Ghost and His angels your way.

Accepting His Grace

With its streets separated by glistening rivers and its spacious skies spiked by regal church spires, Lübeck was a fairytale come alive in my eyes. I spent my months in Lübeck being joyful and excited. There was so much life here to explore and experience, including the mouthwateringly sweet marzipan (almond candy) and stunning architecture. I also served with an amazing redheaded sister named Sister Peterson who was creative and resourceful. (She found an old DDR typewriter in our apartment, got it to function, and wrote letters with it!) There were also many people who left a positive mark on my heart and on my faith.

One warm summer afternoon, Sister Peterson and I caught a train to the other side of town, gliding by rows of bright yellow rapeseed flowers to meet with one of these amazing individuals, Schwester Möller, a middle-aged Asian member who was kind, friendly, and wise. Whenever we met with her, we would laugh and connect like schoolgirls and receive life wisdom from her as if she were our aunt. On that particular day, we sat with her in her white and spacious kitchen with the perfect ocean vibe. (As a huge fan of mermaids, I loved her house!) She had prepared for us a hearty meal of chicken, salad, and potatoes. I politely devoured her food and soaked in the warm, welcoming atmosphere she created. We talked about all kinds of different life topics at her kitchen table, with sunlight streaming through the windows. She advised us, "Always be true to yourself." I left Schwester Möller's home feeling seen and uplifted, and I know she was one of those people God placed in my path to help me grow and feel His love.

After our pleasant lunch with Schwester Möller, Sister Peterson and I had a good half hour before our train would arrive, so I told her, "Let's go walk to the beach with our extra time." She agreed, and we decided to look for people to teach along the way. Eagerly, I started down the sidewalk to the beach, anticipating the spacious sea view and white-tipped waves. Sister Peterson walked alongside me, and before we reached the sand, we found someone to approach about our gospel message.

"Hello!" Sister Peterson and I called out to the woman. "We have a message to share about Jesus Christ."

To my surprise, the woman didn't tell us "no time" or "not interested." (I know, I have such little faith sometimes!) Instead, she said, "I believe in Christ. I'm a Christian." Then she looked at us intensely and asked, "Have you accepted Christ as your Savior?"

Stunned, I stared back at her, feeling like her direct gaze penetrated my soul. I thought to myself, "*Had* I fully accepted Christ as my Savior? I believe in Christ, but do I fully believe that He can help and save me?" A little tongue-tied, I nodded and smiled at the woman as she warmly expressed her love for the Savior and handed me a piece of paper that explained how to accept Christ as your Savior. She said, "You can pray to the Lord and turn your life over to Him."

Her words about accepting Christ as my Savior left an impression on my heart that's still there today. I accepted the paper and thanked the woman. We didn't talk much longer after that, but I never forgot her faith and desire to share what she knew. I felt that God had known

I would choose to walk to the beach, so He sent this woman to help teach me more about His grace.

YOMO Truths: Trusting the Lord

When the faithful woman at the beach peered into my soul and asked, "Have you accepted Christ as your Savior?" I initially responded that I believe in Christ. But like I just mentioned, it got me thinking . . . do I fully believe in Him and His promises to me specifically? As Stephen E. Robinson taught in his book *Believing Christ,* we need to "not only believe in Christ but also believe Him"—that he can save us *personally*.[72] I knew at that moment, and still know, that I can do better in believing the Savior and His promises. As Elder Bednar said, "Believing Him—accepting as true His power and promises—invites perspective, peace, and joy into our lives."[73] We need to not only understand Christ's Atonement but to believe that His Atonement applies to ourselves and our lives. This woman on the beach had faith in Christ and knew Him as her Savior and Redeemer. As she shared her testimony, it was clear that she experienced the joy Elder Bednar described.

From this faithful woman at the beach, I was reminded of our ultimate choice: accepting Christ or not. Christ has already died for us and atoned for our sins, but it's up to us to trust Him, to give Him our heart, to completely accept Him as our Savior, and to accept His blessings. Do we believe in Christ's promises? Elder Robinson, in a BYU address, further explained, "We must not only believe in Christ, [but] we must believe Christ when he says, 'I can cleanse you and make you celestial.'"[74] We need to have faith in Christ that He can empower and perfect us.

Sometimes trusting in the Savior is not easy. It can be difficult to apply His words to ourselves personally. However, I know that Jesus

---

72. Stephen E. Robinson, *Believing Christ: The Parable of the Bicycle and Other Good News* (Salt Lake City, UT: Deseret Book, 1992).
73. David A. Bednar, "If Ye Had Known Me," *Ensign* or *Liahona*, Nov. 2016, 105.
74. Stephen E. Robinson, "Believing Christ: A Practical Approach to the Atonement" (Brigham Young University devotional, May 29, 1990), 2, speeches.byu.edu.

Christ is the Son of God, that He overcame sin and death for every single one of us, and that His arms of mercy are extended to all (see Alma 5:33; 3 Nephi 9:14). Choose to learn more about your Savior and follow and trust Him (see Mosiah 29:20). As you open your heart to Christ and choose to rely on Him, you will experience miracles and great personal growth. He will help you become the missionary and the person you always dreamed of being. That is the promise the Savior offers you when you accept His grace and help.

Understanding His Grace

So what does Christ's grace really mean? How can we access the Savior's grace and help? Elder Bednar explained the difference between the redeeming and enabling powers of the Atonement.[75] He said that when we repent, Christ's redeeming power washes away the effects of sin and makes us clean again. But we often don't realize that Christ's enabling power, or grace, is also available to us. Elder Bednar said, "It is one thing to know that Jesus Christ came to earth to *die* for us. . . . But we also need to appreciate that the Lord desires, through His Atonement and by the power of the Holy Ghost, to *live* in us—not only to direct us but also to empower us."[76]

The Savior wants to redeem us in the next life and strengthen us now. Elder Bednar further explained that Christ's Atonement is not just for "sinners" but also for "saints." Not only can we turn to the Savior when we have done something wrong, but we can turn to the Savior when we are trying to do what is right. Elder Bednar defined this enabling power, or grace, using the Bible Dictionary: "[Grace is] divine means of help or strength. . . . [People] receive strength and assistance to do good works that they otherwise would not be able to maintain if left to their own means."[77]

So grace (or the enabling power of Christ's Atonement) is divine help. It's the strength we need to become our best selves. With the Savior's enabling power, we can do good things we couldn't do by just

---

75. David A. Bednar, "In the Strength of the Lord" (Brigham Young University devotional, October 23, 2001), speeches.byu.edu.
76. David A. Bednar, "In the Strength," 2–3.
77. David A. Bednar, "In the Strength," 3.

relying on our own strength. I was often asked to do things out of my comfort zone on my mission! Some tasks made me feel hesitant, shy, or nervous. At other times, I battled my own feelings of selfishness and laziness. However, every time I prayed for help to finish a task, I was strengthened to serve and work hard. The Lord helped expand my skills as I gave my best effort and prayed for His divine help and grace.

I would like to highlight another principle of the enabling power that Elder Bednar explained: the strength to change our circumstances. He said, "As you and I come to understand and employ the enabling power of the Atonement in our personal lives, we will pray and seek for strength to change our circumstances rather than praying for our circumstances to be changed."[78]

Honestly, I'm not yet at that point in my faith and conversion journey. When things go wrong, my first impulse is to complain like Laman and Lemuel, not pray and be a spiritual giant like Nephi. However, I know that the Savior's enabling power is real and that we can gradually learn more about it and get better at calling on His power to help us accomplish difficult things.

I wanted to share this definition of grace with you—this difference between the redeeming and enabling powers of Christ's Atonement that Elder Bednar described—to let you know that you don't have to do your mission on your own. God will ask you to do hard things, but you can pray for the Savior's grace, His enabling power, to expand your abilities. In Alma 26:12, Ammon, one of the best-known missionaries in the Book of Mormon, bore testimony of the Lord's strength: "Yea, I know that I am nothing; as to my strength I am weak; therefore I will not boast of myself, but I will boast of my God, for in his strength I can do all things."

Sometimes we may feel, like Ammon, that we are weak, but with God's strength, we can do many good things. Sisters, remember that Christ's enabling power is available to you, and His grace will empower you to be the best missionary you can be.

---

78. David A. Bednar, "In the Strength," 4.

Applying His Grace

One resource that has helped me better understand and apply the Savior's Atonement is Brad Wilcox's BYU devotional "His Grace Is Sufficient." I encourage you to read it! Brother Wilcox relates learning the piano to applying the Savior's Atonement. One of my favorite quotes from the talk is how we don't have to be perfect: "There should never be just two options: perfection or giving up. Learning takes time. When we understand grace, we understand that God is long-suffering, that change is a process, and that repentance is a pattern in our lives."[79]

Find comfort in this counsel! We don't have to be perfect—we just need to keep trying. Becoming the disciple we hope to be takes time and effort. It won't happen instantly, like one of my favorite meat-filled microwavable burritos transforming from frozenness to deliciousness in less than five minutes. Instead, it's more like an endless round of homemade Amish friendship bread with multiple ingredients and preparatory hours. We can take steps to change and improve and strive for continuous repentance to help us become like Christ. While such a lengthy process can feel overwhelming, we aren't left to progress on our own. Citing Elder Bruce C. Hafen, Brother Wilcox shared that the Savior's grace can be with us during every stage of our journey.[80] We don't have to reach a certain level of perfection to receive grace; the Savior's grace is always there.

Christ Is with Us

During my mission, I had many ups and downs. Mission life felt like a roller coaster at times! If you experience this, know that it's normal. My dad wrote in a mission letter to me, "Some things will be a struggle, and you will have immense highs and lows as you serve. Expect them and cherish them." There were certain challenges that I struggled with throughout my mission, and I often made mistakes. There were times when I felt discouraged and overwhelmed, but every

---

79. Brad Wilcox, "His Grace Is Sufficient" (Brigham Young University devotional, July 12, 2011), 5, speeches.byu.edu.
80. Brad Wilcox, "His Grace Is Sufficient," 5.

time I fell, the Lord picked me back up. For example, in my tender mercies journal on June 22, 2016, I wrote, "I was upset with others and my own mistakes, but the Spirit comforted me. Knowing that God and Jesus love me and are there for me makes all the difference." I have countless entries similar to the one above—times when the Savior lifted me from sadness and distress to peace and hope.

During one challenge, I remember feeling like the Savior was beside me. I felt like He understood my struggles and weaknesses and comforted me. I know Alma's promise in Alma 7:11–13 to be true:

> And he shall go forth, suffering pains and afflictions and temptations of every kind; and this that the word might be fulfilled which saith he will take upon him the pains and the sicknesses of his people.
>
> And he will take upon him death, that he may loose the bands of death which bind his people; and he will take upon him their infirmities, that his bowels may be filled with mercy, according to the flesh, that he may know according to the flesh how to succor his people according to their infirmities.
>
> Now the Spirit knoweth all things; nevertheless the Son of God suffereth according to the flesh that he might take upon him the sins of his people, that he might blot out their transgressions according to the power of his deliverance; and now behold, this is the testimony which is in me.

Christ will be with you during your times of trial. He will send His Spirit to comfort, uplift, and enlighten you. He knows exactly how you feel and understands and loves you perfectly. Pray and seek His Spirit and help, and you can overcome your trials. Sisters, the Savior loves you, knows who you are, and will be there for you.

My Testimony of Christ

I was in Dresden, an eastern German city, visiting the Frauenkirche. This beautiful Lutheran church had been burned to the ground during World War II, but the Germans had built it back up after the war using some of its original, now blackened stones.[81] It was like a

---

81. See Dieter F. Uchtdorf, "He Will Place You on His Shoulders and Carry You Home," *Ensign* or *Liahona*, May 2016, 101.

phoenix rising out of the ashes. A group of us missionaries walked into the church and sat in a back pew to look up at the divine artwork. The ceiling contained a beautiful and colorful mural. However, what caught my attention the most was a white and golden statue of Christ praying in the Garden of Gethsemane, with His disciples resting and soldiers drawing closer to take him away. Studying the beautiful artwork and reverent scenes, I felt the Spirit so strongly. I felt another witness from the Holy Ghost that Jesus is the Christ, our Savior, that He truly atoned for our sins, and that His Atonement makes all the difference for every human being. Jesus loves us and died for us. He is with us in our trials and wants to help us. We can have His love in our hearts.

I want to add to my testimony with words from my finisher's letter: "The Savior knows what we are going through, and in times of trial He can comfort us. In times of temptation, He can be with us. . . . Jesus Christ can take away the guilt from our hearts (see Alma 24:10–12). The Spirit impressed that truth upon me. What a blessing! . . . The Savior loves each of us and our families. He truly died and suffered for every individual—each one of us—because He loves us." As a missionary, my testimony of Christ and His Atonement grew. I learned about the Savior's grace and forgiveness. He never stops loving us.

YOMO Activity: Reflect On Your Testimony

Write down your testimony of Christ and His gospel. Ponder a time when the Lord has helped you or answered your prayer. Record those experiences in your journal. What can you do to continue to strengthen your faith in the Savior and His grace and enabling power?

Study Session: Accepting Christ and Divine Help

- Dieter F. Uchtdorf, "He Will Place You on His Shoulders and Carry You Home," *Ensign* or *Liahona*, May 2016, 101–4.
- David A. Bednar, "If Ye Had Known Me," *Ensign* or *Liahona*, Nov. 2016, 102–5.

- Linda K. Burton, "Certain Women," *Ensign* or *Liahona*, May 2017, 12–15.

- David A. Bednar, "In the Strength of the Lord" (Brigham Young University devotional, Oct. 23, 2001), speeches.byu.edu.

- Brad Wilcox, "His Grace is Sufficient" (Brigham Young University devotional, July 12, 2011), speeches.byu.edu.

- Stephen E. Robinson, "Believing Christ: A Practical Approach to the Atonement" (Brigham Young University devotional, May 29, 1900), speeches.byu.edu.

- "I Believe in Christ," *Hymns*, no. 134.

- The section "The Savior will support me in my trials" in "Daniel 1–6" (October 31–November 6), *Come, Follow Me—For Individuals and Families: Old Testament 2022*.

- Alma 7:11–13; Doctrine and Covenants 84:88

8

SERVING BEFORE FLIRTING

Trust me, serving *has* to come before flirting.

"The Lord perfectly understands every situation we are in. And He is the one giving us standards to live by."[82]

SERVING BEFORE FLIRTING

Not going to lie, I was *so* awkward before my mission. Like awkward as in socially awkward around boys. I was such a mess! I was too shy to even say hi to a guy, and I never had very many guy friends. For my senior prom, I had to ask a guy from another ward I didn't know because *no one* at my school wanted to go with me. Literally, one guy said he didn't want to go with me "because it would be too awkward since she never talks."

Basically, before my mission, I hadn't had many experiences with boys. Then I became a sister missionary and found myself serving alongside elders my whole mission! It was childish, but I remember checking out all the European elders at the England MTC and

---

82. "Take It from Me: 'Love' Can Wait," *New Era,* Mar. 2016.

crushing on one of the German elders. (No, he didn't serve in the same mission as me.) As I met up with all the other trainees[83] in Freiberg, I was *so* excited by how many boys were around. The odds were even in my favor since there were far more elders than sisters. During dinner one night with all the new missionaries, I remember sashaying around the tables, black skirt flying, hoping the elders were noticing me. (Yes, it's embarrassing even to be writing this, let alone think I was acting so silly on my mission!) I feel like the mission president's wife sensed my flirtatious desires because she pulled me aside that weekend and told me to wear pantyhose or stockings next time. No more flying, flashing bare legs!

However, my romantic inclinations did not change by putting on pantyhose. I couldn't help but notice and enjoy talking with the elders. I wasn't used to talking to boys, and I justified my enjoyment of talking to them by telling myself that it was the mission's fault for making me serve often with the elders. However, I should have been more professional in my interactions with them. Anyway, I remember being so nervous to talk to the elders during those first training meetings, but soon enough, I found myself enjoying it—a bit *too* much.

So not flirting was a struggle for me. I crushed on multiple elders, which I still regret to this day. I regret how I fantasized about certain elders, wanted to talk to them more than anyone else, and set my heart on them instead of on the work. I remember complaining to my companion from South Korea about my struggle with liking elders while trying to remain focused on missionary work. With her usual bluntness and flair, she told me, "You can't chase two rabbits at once. Only one." I hated it when my companions were right. She was totally right. A few nights later, the Spirit sent me a similar message—a feeling that I needed to let go of flirting during my time as a missionary and be more dedicated to the work. I needed to change not only my actions but also my desires and my focus. Although I couldn't deny the strong message from the Spirit, it was hard to act on it. For once, I wasn't awkward. I now knew how to talk to boys. For the girl nobody

---

83. A "trainee" refers to a brand-new missionary who receives extra instruction from a companion called a "trainer."

asked to senior prom, this mattered a great deal to me. What if I gave up flirting and returned home just as awkward as before?

However, I committed to being better and refocused on the work. I stopped fantasizing and stopped seeking out opportunities to flirt. While I still made mistakes, I eventually became the missionary I had always dreamed of becoming: one who was dedicated to the Lord and was confident and joyful as a missionary. Serving, not flirting, helped me YOMO!

Additionally, I gained something far more valuable than flirting skills. During those eighteen months, I gradually discovered the joy of service. I learned firsthand the power of true human connection from teaching people and listening to their stories. I learned that charity, not flirting or popularity, brings true joy. God knew that the lesson I needed to learn even more than flirting was love—the pure love of Christ.

YOMO Truths: Serving Before Flirting

If you're like me, you may wonder about the "why" behind rules like no flirting and dating. As someone who has made mistakes, I can tell you one reason for the no-flirting rule: It will help you keep your heart and mind focused on the work by eliminating romantic distractions. You'll be able to be a more dedicated YOMO missionary.

Maybe refraining from romance won't be a problem for you, but you may struggle with a different rule or challenge. Even when you don't know the reason for a specific guideline, know that missionary rules are inspired by God, and mission presidents sometimes adapt routines to meet the particular needs of different areas. In a *New Era* article, "Take It From Me: 'Love' Can Wait," an anonymous author shared why the dating standards in the *For the Strength of Youth* pamphlet matter: "The Lord perfectly understands every situation we are in. And He is the one giving us standards to live by."[84]

Similarly, Heavenly Father is aware of His missionaries. The rules and guidelines that the prophet, Apostles, and mission leaders set for us are inspired by God. Sometimes it may feel like certain rules are restrictive, but the rules are there to protect us as missionaries. Elder

---

84. "Take It from Me."

Von G. Keetch described how sometimes rules can seem limiting. He shared the story of witnessing a group of American surfers complaining about a barrier in the ocean that prevented them from enjoying the waves on their trip to Australia. Then an older local man gave the group binoculars and showed them that the barrier was actually protecting them from sharks! The Americans suddenly understood the reason for the barrier. Elder Keetch said, "As you and I walk the paths of life and pursue our dreams, God's commands and standards—like the barrier—can sometimes be difficult to understand. They may appear rigid and unyielding, blocking a path that looks fun and exciting and that is being followed by so many others . . . [but] we often cannot comprehend the great dangers hidden just below the surface."[85]

Sometimes it can be hard to follow various rules and standards when the world makes other paths look terribly exciting and enticing. However, what helps me move forward on the covenant path is remembering divine truths, remembering my divine identity, and remembering that many barriers are set in place by our loving Heavenly Father to protect us from dangers and challenges we don't fully understand, as Elder Keetch taught.

On your mission, you will be asked to follow rules and a certain routine. Some of these rules (like not flirting) may be harder to keep than others. Or maybe some rules may seem illogical to you. (I know I was guilty of this—doubting the rules.) However, something amazing happens when we humble ourselves and decide to do things the Lord's way. Just know that many, if not all, rules are set in place to protect you from all sorts of "sharks" and are meant to help guide you to be the best missionary you can be. The heading of Doctrine and Covenants 89 reads, "Obedience to gospel law . . brings temporal and spiritual blessings." As you are obedient, the Lord will bless you. Blessings won't always come in the ways you expect, but you will receive them.

I know from personal experience that following rules isn't always easy. Not flirting was a real challenge for me! However, we will receive great joy as we put the Lord first in our lives and in our missionary

---

85. Von G. Keetch, "Blessed and Happy Are Those Who Keep the Commandments of God," *Ensign* or *Liahona*, Nov. 2015, 116.

service. Heavenly Father knows what is best for us and wants to help us succeed. Listen to the Holy Ghost, who will guide you as you strive to follow the rules and abide by the missionary schedule. As you are meek and seek the Spirit, you will YOMO with more peace and love.

YOMO Tips on Serving Before Flirting:

1. Know that whatever struggle you face on the mission, whatever weakness you are asked to confront, you don't have to do it alone. Our Heavenly Father knows you perfectly and loves you perfectly. Christ will walk with you. Turn to the Savior when you are tempted or fall short. He will not abandon you but will send His Spirit to comfort and uplift you during your challenges.

2. If you're struggling with flirting or having crushes that distract you from the work, inform your mission president. Always follow your mission's rules regarding conduct with other missionaries, members, and people you teach. Striving to obey all the mission rules helps shield you from tempting situations. It's harder to do the wrong thing when you're in the right place striving to do the right thing.

3. When romantic thoughts come, don't suppress them. Instead, acknowledge them as healthy and then move on to thinking about something else. Be patient with yourself as you strive to be focused on the work. With God's help, you can accomplish your righteous goals and become a more Christlike individual and missionary.

4. Seek help from trusted adults if you are struggling with flirting or any other challenge. Don't be afraid to tell your parents or other trusted adults back home about your challenges. Share your joys, but don't hesitate to ask them for their advice and counsel. They want to help you, and they likely know you very well. You don't have to do everything alone.

5. Be aware that sometimes men may try to flirt with you. Know that it's okay to ignore creepy men and leave sketchy situations.

While trusting in God's ability to protect His missionaries, do what you can to avoid unsafe circumstances, such as always staying with your companion and obeying rules regarding curfew.

6. In addition, it's very natural, normal, and healthy to have romantic feelings, especially in your teenage and young adult stages of life. So know that romantic thoughts are not bad. For example, it's okay if you occasionally find someone cute or attractive. The mission is just not the season in your life to focus on romance. (That can come afterward when you can date up a storm if you'd like to!)

7. Please don't feel ashamed if you do struggle with flirting or any other rule. I know the Savior is understanding when we make mistakes or have weaknesses. Elder Richard G. Scott taught that God views weaknesses and rebellion differently. The Lord is merciful with our weaknesses.[86] Imagine the Savior lovingly walking with you and encouraging you on your journey.

From my imperfect experience, I promise that if you do your best to put the Lord and His work first, everything else will fall into place in due time. (And guess what? When I came home from my mission, I was totally able to flirt *way* better than before, but of course, I was still me and had my awkward moments.)

YOMO Challenge: To Flirt or Not to Flirt? To Obey or Not to Obey?

I invite you to act on one of the following options, whichever one speaks to you and your situation the most.

Option 1: Do you get really nervous around guys? If so, it's totally normal, I felt the same way! I've heard that boys get just as nervous around girls, so maybe that's comforting to know. Your challenge: Say hi and start a conversation with a young man you admire or find attractive. Regardless of his reaction, you've succeeded as long as you've said hello!

---

86. Richard G. Scott, "Personal Strength through the Atonement of Jesus Christ," *Ensign* or *Liahona*, Nov. 2013, 83.

Option 2: Is there a gospel topic that confuses you, or that you have questions about? It's okay to have questions. I invite you to research that topic, looking to the scriptures, conference talks, and the Lord in prayer for answers. The Gospel Library app has many helpful resources such as the "Topics and Questions" and "Life Help" sections. Sometimes we aren't meant to know everything in this life, but I've found that we can gain knowledge as we humbly ask and study gospel sources. As you look for answers, focus on what you *do* know and believe (as Church leaders such as Elder Holland have advised),[87] and remember the heart of the gospel message—that Jesus loves you and is your Savior.

Study Session: Serving Before Flirting (and Keeping Other Rules)

- Von G. Keetch, "Blessed and Happy Are Those Who Keep the Commandments of God," *Ensign* or *Liahona*, Nov. 2015, 115–117.

- Sheri L. Dew, "Living on the Lord's Side of the Line" (Brigham Young University devotional, March 21, 2000), speeches.byu.edu.

- Staff and Family Services, "Bridling Your Passions: How to Align Sexual Thoughts and Feelings with the Lord's Expectations," *Ensign*, August 2020.

- Doctrine and Covenants 4:2; 58:2; Mosiah 2:41; Alma 38:12

---

87. Jeffrey R. Holland, "Lord, I Believe," *Ensign* or *Liahona*, May 2013, 93–95.

9

Don't Give Up

There's no final buzzer on your success.

"It's possible to commit no mistakes and still lose. That's not weakness—that's life." —Jean-Luc Picard, Star Trek[88]

Sometimes You Try and Fail, and That's Okay

With its cathedral-pierced sky, shimmering rivers, and grand castle-like gate, Lübeck was a diamond of a city. Many strong, faithful members lived in this city, like the ward mission leader, Bruder Berger, and his wife. Bruder and Sister Berger would invite us missionaries to their home, and we would gather at their dining room table and discuss the work, the needs of the people we taught, and the challenges we faced. And they would give us delicious food too! (Not just snacks but whole meals. My favorite thing I ate with them was their homemade applesauce. So good!) They were the most kind-hearted people.

---

88. "Jean-Luc Picard | Quotes | Quotable Quote," Goodreads, accessed Mar. 1, 2023, https://www.goodreads.com/quotes/8660482-it-is-possible-to-commit-no-mistakes-and-still-lose.

They loved the Lord, and they showered love on us. They felt like our grandparents, and I was happy to serve with them.

I also learned a lot from the Berger family, including lessons from a spiritual thought that Bruder Berger gave. His thought has stuck with me because it was initially so troubling. He shared the story of a man continuously pushing against a huge rock (a Christian narrative with an unknown author).[89] This man pushed and shoved against this boulder, giving his best effort, but it never moved. One day, the man was frustrated and had had enough. He called out to God, exclaiming, "Why are you making me push this rock every single day when it's not moving? I'm making no difference!" To his prayer, God replied, "It's making a difference to you. You are getting stronger by pushing on that rock." Sometimes we may give a task our best effort, but we don't manage to solve the problem or get the results we feel we earned. However, that doesn't mean we failed. Some challenges might be given to us just for our growth. Even if we fail, we can find strength in the struggle.

As a missionary getting rejected daily, this was kind of a downer lesson for me. I wanted to hear stories like "Fourth Floor, Last Door" from President Uchtdorf about how all our hard work will pay off in the end.[90] (The Spirit prompted the missionaries in President Uchtdorf's story to go to a certain building, and they knocked on every door until the last one on the fourth floor, where Harriet Uchtdorf lived.) While God did send miracles my way, I faced a lot of failures and rejections as well. For a girl who thrived off the formula "hard work = success," it was tough for me. I felt that if I worked hard, I should get the reward. I should be able to find people to teach, get baptisms, and so on. But I learned that missionary work is the Lord's work—*His* work and glory (see Moses 1:39)—not mine. A mission leader said that God knows who will and who won't accept His message, but He sends us to everyone so that all His children can hear the message and be given the choice to listen or not.

---

89. "The Unmoved Rock," Bible.org, July 20, 2009, https://bible.org/illustration/unmoved-rock.

90. Dieter F. Uchtdorf, "Fourth Floor, Last Door," *Ensign* or *Liahona*, Nov. 2016, 15–18.

In a city located in eastern Germany in the state of Sachsen, my companion and I had the opportunity to meet with a schoolteacher. She was smart and curious and had a natural love for learning. We taught the missionary lessons to her on hot summer days in her apartment, perched on her kitchen stools as she sat across from us on her couch. She was always attentive and asked lots of questions. In August, we were ecstatic when she agreed to come to the Freiberg Temple open house with us. She was progressing! We were confident she felt the Spirit during the temple tour. After walking through the beautiful, sacred rooms, she told us, "I felt calm inside." We took photos with her afterward and were glad she took the time to come and enjoy the temple tour.

However, after the temple visit in the fall, she abruptly stopped meeting with us. We were outside her apartment when we got a voice message from her saying that she wanted to take a break from lessons. My companion and I felt our stomachs drop. It came as a shock to us since we had felt like she enjoyed the temple tour. We were disappointed. From this experience and several others, I learned that sometimes you can give things your best effort and still fail or get rejected, but that doesn't mean you're a failure. Some things are outside your control. For example, you can do everything right and work super hard, and people may still reject the gospel message because they have agency. That doesn't mean you should give up though. God will reward your hard work and diligence, and you never know who will say yes after a torrent of noes, like with the missionaries in Harriet Uchtdorf's story.[91]

Additionally, the Savior atoned and died for us so that He could pick us up when we fall. As you work hard and face failure and rejection, know that the work you're doing matters and that you're getting stronger in the process. Next time you feel like you're pushing against a rock, remember that the Lord is refining you into the person you can become—the person you are meant to become (see 1 Peter 1:7).

---

91. Dieter F. Uchtdorf, "Fourth Floor, Last Door."

Don't Give Up, and You Will Succeed

During the scorching, humid heat of summer, I was struggling. I felt like a failure of a missionary. I went through stages of feeling discouraged, being lazy, and caring less about the mission rules. Then I made a few mistakes and felt great remorse for not living up to being the missionary I wanted to be. I felt defeated, like a queen without her crown.

After a particularly challenging day when I was chastised for one of my mistakes, my companion and I traveled to a zone training meeting. (I had been flirting too much with an elder, and my mission president privately talked to me about the issue and how to improve moving forward. The counsel was needed, but I didn't handle it well and felt a lot of shame instead of healthy guilt.)

The zone training meeting, held every three months with multiple districts, was held in the chapel in my first area, Freiberg, with the temple next door. Despite being in a peaceful and special place, I felt a torrent of emotions inside me, whirling through my mind and soul like a destructive tornado. I thought to myself, "I can't do this anymore! I can't be a missionary anymore. I'm a failure, and this is too hard. I've made too many mistakes. I am not good enough to be here." As these thoughts bombarded my sad heart, I looked across the room of seated missionaries and gazed at the tall, open windows, my brain screaming at me to jump out a window and escape from the mission. But the thought of my brother preparing to leave for his own mission soon stopped me: I didn't want to impact his mission negatively. So I sat in my chair beside my companion, trying to dispel the quiet storm raging inside me.

At some point during the meeting, one of our zone leaders stood up to talk with us. I felt numb at this point, paralyzed in disappointment by the mistakes I had made, unforgiving, and unsure of how to get rid of the emotional pain I was feeling. But when this zone leader opened his mouth and began to speak, I listened. Every missionary in that room listened. Our zone leader said, "God did not send you here to fail."

His words echoed powerfully through the chapel. It wasn't really the zone leader speaking to us but God speaking to us through the zone leader. Everyone could feel it. The Spirit pricked my heart with hope in that moment. *God did not send me here to fail!* I felt light and peace return to my mind and soul. It was a powerful testimony to me that after the night I felt the lowest, Heavenly Father sent me and my fellow missionaries a glorious assurance of His faith in us. It was like He was speaking to us each individually, saying, "I believe in your potential and have complete faith that you can fulfill the mission I sent you here to fulfill."

The zone leader's words, "God did not send you here to fail," taught me to try again rather than give up. After this sacred spiritual experience, I still stumbled. I still struggled with the mistakes I had made and the weaknesses I continued to wrestle with. However, with God's help, I kept trying, and I was able to learn and improve. You will succeed when you don't give up and when you accept God's help. Heavenly Father has not destined you to fail but to triumph gloriously. As President Monson taught, "Our responsibility is to rise from mediocrity to competence, from failure to achievement. Our task is to become our best selves. One of God's greatest gifts to us is the joy of trying again, for no failure ever need be final."[92]

In sports, the game is over when the final buzzer sounds. But during this life, and in God's eyes, there is no such buzzer. We are never thrown out of the game, and the Savior never throws in the towel on us. Christ is our perfect coach, pushing us to become our best selves, picking us up when we're down, and never losing hope in us. Don't give up, because you have a perfect coach by your side. With Him, you will ultimately succeed.

YOMO Truths: Don't Give Up

During another particularly impactful zone conference, my mission leaders showed us a clip about Derek Redmond, an Olympic runner for Great Britain who was no stranger to trials. In the 1992 Olympics held in Barcelona, Redmond was running a race on the track when his right hamstring muscle tore. He was overcome with pain, but before the medical team could reach him, he got up and started jogging and limping, determined to finish the race. As his pain

---

92. Thomas S. Monson, "The Will Within," *Ensign*, May 1987, 68.

grew, his father rushed out onto the track and helped him get to the finish line, which Redmond then crossed, completing the race.[93]

When the mission leaders showed us the video, I teared up a little. I loved running and sports, and Redmond's video really resonated with me. Despite not being an Olympic athlete or having experienced a muscle tear, I could imagine the pain Redmond must have felt when he got injured in the middle of the race—in the middle of his goal, his dream, to which he had dedicated years of preparation. Even as a bystander watching, that kind of heartbreak felt shattering.

I empathized with Redmond because I felt like there were times on the mission when I was spiritually limping, just trying to finish the race like him. I got even more emotional seeing how Redmond's father ran to him and supported him. It felt like a testimony of how the Savior runs to us, ready to support and help us. He will come to us as we fall and fail and face disappointments. We will not be left comfortless (see John 14:18). That means the Savior literally can send us feelings of love, joy, and peace as we let Him and ask Him to do so. Watching the video of Redmond—his failure and pain, his father's support, and, ultimately, his determination not to give up—gave me hope and courage to keep going. The message of the zone conference from mission leaders and the Spirit was "If you don't give up, you will not fail."

However, that doesn't mean you won't ever experience setbacks, which are a normal part of life. Redmond experienced a setback but chose not to give up, and with his father by his side, he finished the race. Similarly, you may fall short sometimes, but if you don't give up, you will succeed in your life's mission with the Savior by your side. The Savior will walk with you, run with you, and even carry you. As you pray and ask for His help, comfort, and enabling power and exercise faith in Him, you will notice Him walking with you.

YOMO Tips on Not Giving Up

1. **Learn how to deal with failure positively.** As mentioned in chapter three, I struggle with perfectionism, so I view failure

---

93. "Derek Redmond," Olympics.com, accessed July 25, 2024, https://olympics.com/en/athletes/derek-redmond.

as a negative reflection of my character. However, as many people have told me, failure is a natural part of our learning process.[94] I challenge you to give yourself more grace. You will fail sometimes as a missionary, so come prepared with strategies that will help you deal with setbacks in a way that is healthy and kind to yourself.

2. **Do hard things.** Don't shy away from doing hard things—before, during, and after your mission! Set goals and go after your dreams, even if it isn't easy. Work hard and celebrate your accomplishments.

3. **Set realistic goals.** Having unrealistic standards and expectations for yourself can lead to burnout, which can lead to feelings of failure and exhaustion. As I mentioned in chapter three, make SMART (specific, measurable, achievable, relevant, time-bound) goals and strive to develop healthy expectations about your performance as a missionary.

4. **Practice self-care.** It's okay to take breaks and to take care of yourself! Pay attention to your stress levels and take action to reduce your stress or your companion's stress. Don't put too much on your plate at once, and take care of your physical and mental health to avoid burnout.

5. **Do more than endure.** I once got called out by my trainee that I need to not just "endure to the end of my mission" but also find joy in it. It may be challenging to fully enjoy the mission at times, but my companion was right. Don't develop an attitude like me to "gut it out" and just get the work done. "Enduring to the end" is not about gritting your teeth until you cross the finish line—it's about having faith and hope in Christ and seeing the positive things around you. Turn to mission leaders and trusted adults when needed, turn to Christ in prayer, and YOMO by finding small things to enjoy each day.

---

94. Amanda Ruggeri, "The Dangerous Downsides of Perfectionism," BBC Future, Feb. 20, 2018, https://www.bbc.com/future/article/20180219-toxic-perfectionism-is-on-the-rise.

YOMO Activity: Self-Care

Practice self-care! Take a break this week and do something to rejuvenate your mind and body, such as getting your nails done, watching an episode of your favorite show, journaling, catching up with an old friend, going on a walk, or doing some other activity that allows you to care for yourself that you consider beneficial.

Study Session: Not Giving Up

- NBC Sports, "Father's Day Lookback: Derek Redmond 1992 | NBC Sports," YouTube, June 16, 2019, https://youtu.be/ynhD-vq2DUE?si=xroXnJHnz23Nt_hx.

- The Church of Jesus Christ of Latter-day Saints, "Your Great Adventure: Overcoming Life's Obstacles," YouTube, Feb. 11, 2021, https://youtu.be/fB0AylSalFs?si=ThZcSOAf0-cjhN21.

- L. Tom Perry, "How to Endure to the End," *New Era*, June 2012, 48.

- Mary N. Cook, "Never, Never, Never Give Up!," *Ensign* or *Liahona*, May 2010, 117–19.

- Kevin J. Worthen, "Successfully Failing: Pursuing Our Quest for Perfection" (Brigham Young University devotional, Jan. 6, 2015), speeches.byu.edu.

- Doctrine and Covenants 14:7; 2 Nephi 31:20; Helaman 5:12

10

THE POWER OF AGENCY

"There is no fate but what we make for ourselves."[95]

"And the Messiah cometh in the fulness of time, that he may redeem the children of men from the fall. And because that they are redeemed from the fall they have become free forever, knowing good from evil; to act for themselves and not to be acted upon, save it be by the punishment of the law at the great and last day, according to the commandments which God hath given." —2 Nephi 2:26

LESSONS FROM MISSING A TRAIN

So it's probably just the fairytale-loving American girl in me, but I must confess that I view train transportation as magical. It's likely related to the fact that I watched the Harry Potter movies one too many times, with the Hogwarts Express faithfully chugging through enchanting European scenery to reach the school castle. Of course,

---

95. "Terminator 2: Judgement Day, 1991 | Linda Hamilton: Sarah Connor," IMDb, accessed July 25, 2024, https://www.imdb.com/title/tt0103064/characters/nm0000157.

in Germany, trains are simply a normal part of everyday life. With Germany's train system, the Deutsche Bahn, you can efficiently travel throughout the country and go from state to state and city to city.

In Zwickau, a city in the state of Sachsen, I served with an amazing missionary named Sister Brown. She was hardworking, athletic, and practical. She was the exact kind of companion I needed at the time! One snowy afternoon, Sister Brown and I decided to visit a family in a nearby village. We grabbed our bags and bundled up in our thick winter coats, stylish scarves, and warm hats and headed out the front door. Despite the frigid gust of wind that greeted us, I was delighted to travel since we would have an hour-and-a-half train ride! Trains just had a way of making me feel like there was adventure just around the corner.

After our train arrived at the village's small station, we trudged downhill through the thick snow. My face and hands tingled with cold. Thankfully, the family we were visiting welcomed us with open arms into their warm, cozy home. We enjoyed our time with the family so much that we lost track of time. The wintry afternoon turned into an even colder and darker evening. Finally, Sister Brown realized how late it was and that our train was about to leave without us! Since we were in a village, trains came and went less frequently than in larger cities. If we missed our train, we would get home past our curfew.

Being as polite as possible, we rushed out of the family's home and into the dark, cold night. Sister Brown started sprinting, so I had no choice but to run. We flew across the snowy sidewalks of the sleepy village. I am surprised neither of us slipped and fell at any point. Sister Brown was determined to catch that train and make that curfew! Being what I consider a fast runner, I could keep up with her, just a few paces behind. However, the train was already there when we approached the hill leading up to the platform. It was going to be a close call, and as Sister Brown kept pressing forward, I began to doubt if we would make it. I thought to myself, "Would it really be that bad if we didn't make it? We would just be late for curfew, which isn't that big of a deal." I definitely should have had a less apathetic and more obedient attitude about curfew, but I didn't. I shouted to Sister Brown, "Hey, we aren't going to make it!" Each step felt so heavy with my solid boots entrenched in deep snow. I felt as exhausted as a marathon runner at the end of a race. "It wouldn't be the end of the world if we miss the train," I thought. That's when I decided to give up. I stopped running, forcing my companion to slow down too. We got to the platform and watched the train smoothly glide away without us into the dark countryside.

For a moment, we were both silent. Then, to my surprise, Sister Brown said something that has stuck with me forever. She said, "Sister Shoaf, I'm not mad that we missed the train, but I am upset that you just gave up." Her earnest, direct gaze held my attention, and I apologized. Being a kind and loyal friend, she forgave me. We shivered as we huddled on the platform, and after a considerable wait, we embarked on our journey home on the next train, with dark fields streaming past our fogged windows.

Looking back, I realize it wasn't about missing or catching trains but about choices and agency. Sister Brown always had a gift for seeing the potential in me, and she knew I could have chosen differently. Maybe we actually could have caught the train if I had run harder, or maybe we still would've missed it. But the fact is, I sealed our fate by giving up. That snowy night, Sister Brown taught me that we are all agents who have the power to act. As 2 Nephi 2:26 teaches, we are meant to act for ourselves and "not to be acted upon." Sister Brown's reprimand rattled me and has stayed with me because I too often forget the power of agency. We are not designed to give up or fall prey to our circumstances. We can control our attitude and our actions. Agency is a principle of power! Although we cannot control outcomes, I have found that often what we make up in our minds does become reality.

With the train adventure, I saw the terrifying hill ahead and assumed I couldn't reach the insurmountable goal of catching the train. I also wasn't burning with the desire to push myself, catch the train, and be on time. On your mission and throughout your life, overwhelming obstacles and seemingly impossible goals will appear before you. Instead of choosing fear and apathy like I did, turn to God and act. As I mentioned earlier in this book, "Pray as though everything depended on God; work as though everything depended on you"

(St. Augustine).[96] Remember that you are an agent. You can act and change your circumstances and yourself with God's help. Don't underestimate yourself and the good that you can do.

YOMO Truths: Be an Agent

To fully harness the power of agency, it's essential to understand its meaning first. The Guide to the Scriptures defines agency as "the ability and privilege God gives people to choose and to act for themselves."[97] Sometimes we forget this capacity that we have to create change and improve our lives. I know that I'm often guilty of seeing situations as happening *to* me, feeling more like I'm "being acted upon," and forgetting that I'm meant "to act" (see 2 Nephi 2:14, 26). Sometimes things are outside of our control, but we can determine our course of action.

I'd like to review the story of Esther from the Old Testament. Not only is the account of Esther cool because it includes a female protagonist, but her story is a great example of the principle of agency. Let's see what we can learn from her about being an agent instead of an object.

A long time ago, King Ahasuerus of Persia was looking for a new wife after dismissing his former queen, Vashti. (Interestingly, Vashti is an example of being an agent as well because when the king wanted to show off her beauty to drunk men, she refused to obey his request. See Esther 1:10–12.) To find a new queen, King Ahasuerus commanded that all the young virgins in the land be presented to him. He chose Esther, a beautiful woman raised by her uncle named Mordecai. Esther was also a Jew, and Mordecai told her to keep her identity a secret. After his niece became queen, Mordecai offended Haman, a man recently promoted to more power, by not bowing to him. When Haman discovered that Mordecai was a Jew, he presented to King Ahasuerus a plan to eliminate all Jews from the land. The king agreed to the plan, and messengers sent the decree out to kill all Jews.

---

96. Saint Augustine, "Saint Augustine Quotes," Brainy Quote, accessed July 25, 2024, https://www.brainyquote.com/quotes/saint_augustine_165165.
97. Guide to the Scriptures, "Agency," Gospel Library.

Mordecai learned of the plot and sent a letter to Esther, pleading with her to go to the king and stand up for her people. Esther replied that it was dangerous for her to speak to the king, her husband, because he had not invited her to see him for thirty days, and anyone who went to the king in the inner court without being called upon was killed unless he offered that person the golden scepter (see Esther 2–4). Mordecai then responded, "Think not with thyself that thou shalt escape in the king's house, more than all the Jews. For if thou altogether holdest thy peace at this time, then shall there enlargement and deliverance arise to the Jews from another place; but thou and thy father's house shall be destroyed: and who knoweth whether thou art come to the kingdom for such a time as this?" (Esther 4:13–14).

This is when Esther acted as an agent. Instead of becoming immobilized by fear, she decided to heed her uncle's request. Esther replied, "Go, gather together all the Jews that are present in Shushan, and fast ye for me, and neither eat nor drink three days, night or day: I also and my maidens will fast likewise; and so will I go in unto the king, which is not according to the law: and if I perish, I perish" (Esther 4:16).

Esther understood the risk she was about to take by going in to see the king uninvited. However, she courageously stepped into the king's inner court, and King Ahasuerus handed her the golden scepter. Esther then invited the king to a banquet and then to a second banquet, where she exposed Haman as the enemy of her people. King Ahasuerus loved Esther, so he had Haman hanged, and he granted Esther's wish to save her people. He allowed her to send out letters in his name to reverse the decree against the Jews. The Jewish people conquered their enemies and celebrated (see Esther 5–8).

So what can we learn from Esther's story? First, Esther was an agent. She didn't just let things happen to her—she took matters into her own hands while trusting God. When Esther went to save her people, she fasted and prayed *and* acted, courageously stepping into the king's hall. Esther chose faith over fear, accepted Mordecai's call to serve her people, and did what she could, leaving the rest to God. Like Esther, we can be agents and remember that we can act, change, and create change. You have influence! You matter. You can change your life and positively impact other people's lives. Remember the power of agency on your mission, and YOMO!

YOMO Story: Don't Blame God

One sunny afternoon in the beautiful cobblestone streets of Lübeck, I approached a woman and invited her to learn more about the gospel of Christ. She was older and gave off intellectual vibes. While she wasn't interested in learning more about the gospel, she was willing to talk with me about the principle of agency. I found her words electrifying. She said, "We shouldn't blame God for everything bad in our life. We need to follow the feelings of our heart and take responsibility for our mistakes."

As a missionary, we talk to many people, and that conversation was one of the few that ingrained themselves in my memory. In my mission letter to myself, I wrote about what agency meant to me: "We have the power to act. We are agents. We determine our destiny. If you are in a hard situation, *do* something to change it! We control who we become." For the girl prone to complaining or vacillating between decisions, it's empowering to hear that I can create change in my life.

However, it's important to note that while we can control who we become, we can't control every circumstance of our lives. Additionally, certain challenges, such as those involving poverty, illness, disability, or abuse, are hard to overcome. In such conditions, altering the situation may be impossible or extremely difficult. However, we can always strive for hope. We can change what is in our control and have faith and patience for what is outside our control (which is admittedly easier said than done). While we can't always change everything about our lives, isn't it empowering to know that we always get to make the next move? As President Uchtdorf said, "It is your reaction to adversity, not the adversity itself, that determines how your life's story will develop."[98] Take charge of your life story, sisters, with heaven cheering you on!

---

98. Dieter F. Uchtdorf, "Your Happily Ever After," *Ensign* or *Liahona*, May 2010, 126.

Reflection Questions

1. Do you sometimes blame God for the bad things that happen in your life? What can you do instead when challenges come?
2. How can you choose faith over fear like Esther?
3. How can you rely on God and take action at the same time?
4. From this chapter, what have you learned about being an agent?

Study Session: Be an Agent

- Gospel Topics, "Agency and Accountability," Gospel Library.
- Joy D. Jones, "Look unto Him in Every Thought" (Brigham Young University devotional, Aug. 21, 2018), speeches.byu.edu.
- D. Todd Christofferson, "Moral Agency" (Brigham Young University devotional, Jan. 31, 2006), speeches.byu.edu.
- David A. Bednar, "Things to Act and Things to be Acted Upon" (video), Gospel Library.
- "Having Courage & Trusting the Lord: Stand Up for What You Believe In" (video), Gospel Library.
- The Book of Esther in the Old Testament
- 2 Nephi 2; Helaman 14:30; Joshua 24:15; Doctrine and Covenants 29:39

11

SERVICE SAVES SOULS

It still surprises me how service is always the answer.

"Forget yourself and go to work."
—*Bryant Stringham Hinckley, President Hinckley's father*

SAVED BY SERVICE

On a bright and crisp fall day in a countryside village, I got to help mentor a youth and teach her about missionary work. It was one of the most joyful experiences of my mission! My companion and I traveled about forty minutes from our area, Chemnitz, to participate in the stake's Youth Missionary Weekend in Schwarzenberg. We were both elated at the opportunity to travel and be part of this exciting activity. Once we arrived at the chapel in Schwarzenberg, the stake leaders paired each missionary, both sisters and elders, with a youth of the same gender. I got paired with a recent convert, a sweet sixteen-year-old named Alina, who had been baptized by a former elder from Indiana, my home state. It felt like a perfect pairing. The local leaders instructed me to show her the ropes of missionary work. I was to spend half the day with her, walking her through the daily life of a missionary. First, we studied the scriptures together in the chapel. Then we went out to the village and went finding together.

Usually, finding was something that stressed me out. I didn't look forward to it because it felt intimidating to me to approach people on the street and start talking to them about religion. However, today I wasn't as focused on my worries as I usually was because I was more concerned about giving Alina a "real missionary moment" to help her have at least one conversation with someone about the gospel. We hit the street, eager to work.

As Alina and I walked down the hilly path to the village, I couldn't help but feel giddy at the beauty of the scene before us. We were surrounded by rich and hilly farmland and majestic forests whose sturdy trees pierced the sky in the distance. In my email home to my family, I wrote, "We went finding in Schwarzenberg, which is a small Dorf—a village—with a castle and a church and hills and trees . . . and I about died because I *love* the German countryside!" Not only did it feel amazing to be back in the country, but there was a peaceful vibe in the fresh air as Alina and I connected with one another and invited people to learn about the gospel of Christ. Alina was bright and warm and enjoyable to be with, and although I was trying to teach her, I also learned from her about being enthusiastic and full of faith. Eventually, we found our way onto a dirt path that led to a rustic house above the main village. We knocked, and a lady answered! Our conversation went something like this:

"Hello!" I said, "We're missionaries for The Church of Jesus Christ of Latter-day Saints. Can we tell you a little more about our faith?"

To my surprise and excitement, the woman replied, "Yes, you can tell me more about your faith."

We shared what we believed with her, about God and His plan for us. Alina and I had a good conversation with this woman, and I felt satisfied that I—well, Heavenly Father really—gave Alina a little missionary experience.

After returning to the chapel, the missionaries and youth held a testimony meeting. In my tender mercies journal, I wrote, "I felt the Spirit strongly during the testimony meeting, and I know this gospel is true—and today I know and feel that it is good news! Joy!" After the meeting, I enjoyed talking to a couple of the leaders from

Schwarzenberg. Everyone was feeling the spirit of missionary work and the joy of the gospel of Christ. Beaming with excitement and gratitude, I boarded the train home with my companion. I was glad I got paired with Alina and enjoyed mentoring her.

That was the lesson for me from the spiritually invigorating Youth Missionary Weekend in Schwarzenberg: Serve and focus on others, and you will be a happier and more successful missionary! My previous companion in Chemnitz had written in my Tschüss Buch (the scrapbook we Berlin missionaries would make, filled with pictures and letters from our companions) that the best mission advice she could give was from President Hinckley's father: "Forget yourself and go to work."[99] I learned that one of the easiest ways to forget yourself is to focus more on others. For me, that meant serving others and trying to think about their needs instead of overthinking my problems and focusing on my fears. On the mission, whenever I was in my own head, my encounters with members and strangers got more awkward. I felt more self-conscious and did more cringey things! However, when I focused on service, I was happier and more confident in my interactions with others. I was so happy in Schwarzenberg that day, not just because that village has a glorious countryside but also because I was more focused on Alina's happiness than my own, which I must confess is rare for me. Whenever I strove to serve and connect with people, everything about my life as a missionary felt happier and lighter. Service will save you on the mission and help you reach your full potential as a disciple of Christ.

Joy of Service

In a charming city in Thüringen during the last few months of my mission, my companion, Sister Grace, and I were living up our YOMO transfer. We ran to catch trains, enjoyed preparation days by exploring castles, and had fun street displays with the members and other missionaries in the area. I enjoyed being with Sister Grace, who reminded me of one of my best friends back home. She was kind, thoughtful, beautiful, and willing to go along with my crazy plans. It was a happy time, although we struggled to find people to teach,

---

99. *Teachings of Presidents of the Church: Gordon B. Hinckley* (2016), 8.

which is why we were elated when a very old and sweet woman named Schwester Neumann welcomed us into her home one afternoon.

Schwester Neumann had straight gray hair and kind eyes that had seen a lot of years of life and undoubtedly many trials, but she had a friendly and warm light about her. When we knocked on her apartment door, she welcomed us in and was very receptive to the gospel message. Unfortunately, she suffered from some form of memory loss, asking for our names multiple times. However, she listened as we taught her about the First Vision, when Joseph Smith prayed to know which church to join and Heavenly Father and Jesus Christ appeared to him. I read to her from Joseph Smith History 1:16–17—"I saw a pillar of light exactly over my head, above the brightness of the sun. . . . I saw two Personages whose brightness and glory defy all description"—and my companion and I testified of gospel truths being restored again to the earth.

Schwester Neumann listened, and as we invited her to share what she was thinking, she confessed, "I didn't really understand what you were saying, but I didn't want to interrupt because I liked how you said it."

I interpreted that to mean that besides my German language skills needing more work, Schwester Neumann had felt the Holy Ghost! Sister Grace and I felt the Spirit strongly as well. We offered her a Book of Mormon, and she accepted it and said, "I've always wanted one."

We hugged her and promised to come back soon, and then we stepped into the warm summer evening with hopeful hearts and gratitude for the lesson and the Spirit we were able to share with that special sister.

The following week, we attempted to visit Schwester Neumann. We even brought a member with us, but she wasn't home. Undeterred, Sister Grace thought we should try again, so we went by her home a few days later, and Schwester Neumann again warmly welcomed us into her home. However, she didn't remember us at all! I was disappointed, but I could still feel a kind spirit about her. Sister Grace noticed her house was a bit dirty and asked, "Can we come back again and clean your bathroom?" Schwester Neumann replied, "Thank you, but I don't need help. I have been cleaning and cooking for years. See, here are pictures of my children," and she commenced showing us family pictures, declaring that she was a proud German housewife.

Sister Grace felt led by the Spirit that we should still serve her, so a few days later, we showed up with yellow sponges, rags, and mops. We cleaned Schwester Neumann's bathroom. (I bravely allowed Sister Grace to tackle the toilet.) After our efforts, the bathroom did look improved, and I think Schwester Neumann appreciated our help. I will never forget her kind smile. Although her memory deficiency prevented her from learning more about the gospel in this life, I feel confident that she will accept the fulness of Christ's gospel in the heavens.

Looking back on this experience, what stands out the most is that God knew Schwester Neumann's circumstances. He knew she would not be able to remember all the lessons, but He still sent us to her. The Spirit also prompted Sister Grace to have us go back and clean her house. This showed me that Heavenly Father cares about each one of us so much. Sometimes He will send us somewhere to brighten someone's day. Or to help them. Or to just listen to them. As missionaries, we should always be teaching and looking for opportunities to teach, but God will also send us to people to simply help them feel His love. He will do this throughout our lives. This is proof of Heavenly Father's perfect love for each of His children.

Sisters, as you reach out and serve with love, you may plant a seed that another missionary or member will eventually harvest. Sometimes your service and kindness will lead you to find a new person to teach. However, even when an individual chooses not to learn more, know it's never a waste to spread Christlike love and light through service. "Remember the worth of souls is great in the sight of God" (Doctrine and Covenants 18:10). Heavenly Father wants us to help other people feel His love, and He wants you to feel His love too. Charity and service will bring you the greatest joy in your mission and throughout your life.

YOMO Truths: Serve!

Service is one of the number one ways to have a YOMO mission! Nothing brings more joy. Because service is one of the main elements of a mission, I'd like to explain a little bit about the "why" of service and the different ways we can serve as missionaries.

First, service is an integral part of your purpose as a missionary. As missionaries, we are literally "called to serve." Additionally, as disciples of Christ, we promised at baptism to serve others throughout our lives. In Mosiah 18:8–10, Alma invited the people (who chose to listen to his gospel message instead of the words of King Noah's wicked priests) to be baptized. He taught them that following the Lord means helping people during times of trial, being there for others when they're sad, and offering reassurance and support. King Benjamin in the Book of Mormon also reminds us that "when ye are in the service of your fellow beings ye are only in the service of your God" (Mosiah 2:17). Your mission can help set a foundation of service for your life.

Now that we've talked about the "why" of service, I'd like to share a little bit about the "how" of service. For me, this is the hard part. I have to confess that I'm not the best at serving. Helping people doesn't always come naturally to me, and I'm not the greatest at noticing needs. However, we don't have to wait to serve until we're superstars at it. We can start where we are. For me, that looked like praying for charity, focusing on others more when talking with them, and making a daily effort to help someone. Although I was imperfect as I strove to serve, Heavenly Father magnified my efforts and blessed me with greater love for the people.

That brings me to my next point: The "how" of service, or the manner or attitude in which you reach out to others, matters. Elder Hartman Rector Jr said, "I long ago learned what all real missionaries must learn: 'People do not really care how much you know until they know how much you care.'"[100]

Your main purpose as missionaries is to invite people to Christ, and it helps if you invite them with Christlike love. Serve, teach, and invite friends of the Church with the fruits of the Spirit: love, joy, peace, longsuffering, gentleness, goodness, faith, meekness, and temperance (see Galatians 5:22–23). People will feel the Spirit through your love and kindness and notice something different. As my dad explained in his mission letter to me, "You don't convert—the Spirit does. So show the fruits of the gospel and people will feel the Spirit, and that influence will change their hearts." Seek to have the Spirit

---

100. Hartman Rector Jr., "You Shall Receive the Spirit," *Ensign,* Nov. 1973, 107.

with you as you serve and teach. Care for the people you teach like you would a friend.

We've learned that missionary work is about serving God's children—inviting them to learn more about His gospel with charity and love—but what does service really look like on a mission? As missionaries, your main goal is to bring others closer to Christ by teaching them His gospel and helping them make covenants. Serving others looks like praying for friends of the Church, thoughtfully planning lessons, and teaching with the Spirit.

While your focus will be on spiritually helping your brothers and sisters, you can physically or temporally serve them as well. With your companion, other missionaries, or ward members, you can participate in service projects at church or in the community. This is a great way to build connections with others, and it can soften hearts and lead to curiosity or a willingness to learn more about the Church. There are lots of ways you can reach out to others. For example, you can help fix lawns and gardens, bake treats, make homemade cards, and be a good listener. Follow the promptings of the Spirit. There are numerous creative ways to show Christlike love.

While service should be done with the intent to help others, it does bring *you* blessings as well. When I was sad or feeling defeated on my mission, service was the number one solution that brought me added courage and peace. In my finisher's letter, I wrote, "Service saves you. When I was drowning, just serving someone—being with and helping others—helped me feel better. Every. Single. Time. Service is your antidote—focus on others and give them God's love." A mission gives you plenty of opportunities to serve because you are basically giving the Lord eighteen months of your life. This kind of dedication brings immense personal growth and blessings.

One message I'd like to highlight about the blessings of service comes from President Spencer W. Kimball. He taught that service enriches our life. He said that serving allows us to focus more on others, which means we worry about our problems less and often have a new perspective on what troubles us after serving. He cited Matthew 10:39 and explained, "The more we serve our fellowmen in appropriate ways, the more substance there is to our souls. . . . Indeed, it is easier to 'find' ourselves because there is so much more of us to find!"[101]

I love President Kimball's message. So many blessings come from service! It's comforting that when we help others, we feel more peace as we focus less on our problems. I also love the promise that as we "lose ourselves" in service, we "find ourselves." It sounds so contradictory, but as a missionary, I learned it's true. The more I strove to serve, the more I grew and learned new things about myself. I felt comforted and less worried about my challenges. Sisters, as you serve, you'll be a happier and more confident YOMO missionary.

YOMO Service Activity

1. Read the talk "He Asks Us to Be His Hands" by Sister Cheryl A. Esplin.

2. Test out the story about mirrors and windows with a group, like Sister Heaston described. Discuss the following questions:

    - How hard is it to talk to someone when looking in a mirror?

    - Why does it work better to speak to someone through a window?

    - Our society often teaches us to be focused on mirrors. How can we put aside our mirrors (including our phones, problems, and insecurities) to look through windows (focusing on other people) and serve?

3. Discuss the following quote from Sister Esplin's talk:

"We were able to see that the young woman had become [her] focal point and that true service requires that we focus on the needs and emotions of others. Ofttimes we are so worried about ourselves and our own busy lives—as we look in mirrors while trying to look

---

101. Garrett H. Garff, "Spencer W. Kimball: Man of Action," *Ensign*, Jan. 2007, 50.

for opportunities to serve—that we do not see clearly through the windows of service."[102]

Sisters, remember to serve with charity and love. As you strive to lose yourself in service to others, you will experience a remarkable YOMO mission!

Study Session: Service

- Cheryl A. Esplin, "He Asks Us to be His Hands," *Ensign* or *Liahona*, May 2016, 6–9.

- Cristina B. Franco, "The Joy of Unselfish Service," *Ensign* or *Liahona*, Nov. 2018, 55–57.

- The section "Missionary Service and Personal Conversion" in "The Life and Ministry of Gordon B. Hinckley," *Teachings of Presidents of the Church: Gordon B. Hinckley* (2016), 6–9.

- Sondra Heaston, "Keeping Your Fingers on the PULSE of Service" (Brigham Young University devotional, June 23, 2015), speeches.byu.edu.

- "Reaching Out With Love" (video), Gospel Library.

- Mosiah 2:17–19; Matthew 16:25; Matthew 10:39; Doctrine and Covenants 4

---

102. Cheryl A. Esplin, "He Asks Us to Be His Hands," *Ensign* or *Liahona*, May 2016, 6–7.

12

Working with Members

The members are like peanut butter to your chocolate, french fries to your shake, and chicken to your waffles: a perfect pairing.

"Now is the time for members and missionaries to come together, to work together, to labor in the Lord's vineyard to bring souls unto Him." —President Thomas S. Monson[103]

How Not to Work with Members: A Cautionary Tale

During Sister Grace's and my YOMO transfer, each day felt like an adventure, and a significant part of that adventure was the people. It was exciting to meet new people, and it was fulfilling to develop relationships with friends of the Church and the brothers and sisters in the ward. We loved the members in our area! They were essential in the work of salvation, helping us with street displays and joint

---

103. Thomas S. Monson, "Welcome to Conference," *Ensign* or *Liahona*, Nov. 2013, 4.

teaching (meaning they went with us to teach a lesson to a friend of the Church, sometimes called "member lessons"). They were amazing! However, in Thüringen, due to my own mistake, I learned an important lesson about how *not* to work with members. It involved soccer and side-tackling an older man.

It was my second-to-last transfer, and I was motivated to make every minute count. I felt regret about my past mistakes and how I had let fear, doubt, and laziness rule the earlier months of my mission, and I was determined to end on a high note. With this mindset, I felt that I needed to be selective about the activities Sister Grace and I engaged in.

In the ward in our area, there was a kind gentleman named Bruder Krüger. He was friendly and athletic and adored soccer. More than once, he invited Sister Grace and me to play soccer with him and some of the members of the ward on Saturday mornings. I remember just smiling at him and saying, "We'll come sometime." However, I was hesitant about joining the men for their soccer games because it seemed unproductive, especially because I love sports and felt like I'd get too distracted if I played. I thought, "This is supposed to be my productive, super-consecrated transfer, and I think I'd have too much fun playing soccer. And what would be the point? We should focus solely on finding." However, Sister Grace figured we should play since Bruder Krüger had invited us so many times, so I agreed that we could participate in the soccer game the following Saturday.

It was a hot summer day when Sister Grace and I walked onto the dirt field, sporting our athletic gear, which consisted of T-shirts and shorts. Bruder Krüger grinned at us, rushed over, and handed us neon-yellow jerseys. Included in the group were mostly older men but also some younger boys, and both members and friends of members played. Sister Grace and I were the only women. (Girl power!)

The game started, and Sister Grace and I played with enthusiasm. While I can't say we had the most skill, we definitely had a lot of fun! I was excited to finally play soccer in Germany, where soccer was such an important part of the culture. Everyone laughed and enjoyed themselves during the game. I have to confess I got a little too competitive though. At some point in the middle of the game, I saw the black-and-white ball up ahead. Sweating and grunting, I lunged for it, only to accidentally side-tackle an old man! I didn't mean to, of course, but I basically went all-in for the ball, wiped out a guy, and got my hand scratched up. Oops! But it was all in good spirits. Bruder Krüger thanked us for coming, and I left, a little banged up but so grateful that we got to have that experience with both members and their friends.

A few days later, I got transferred to a new city. However, the Sunday before I left, Bruder Krüger approached me, and with sincerity, he said, "Thank you for coming to play soccer with us. At first, I was disappointed and upset with you because you kept saying every Sunday that you would come to play with us, but you never did. Then you came. Thank you for coming, Sister Shoaf. Here is a magnet to remember [the area] by." He then offered me a magnet of the city's stunning cathedral and said goodbye. It was a parting gift of friendship, a token of his forgiveness and love. I was grateful I had listened to my companion and played soccer!

From this experience—the mistake I made that was rectified by Sister Grace's wisdom—I learned a valuable lesson about working with members. Being the clueless person I sometimes am, I had absolutely no idea before our last conversation that Bruder Krüger was frustrated with me. I hadn't realized that it would be such a big deal whether I played a game of soccer or not. However, I finally understood that it was about giving my word. I had said I'd play soccer but didn't show up. By not keeping my word, how could I expect Bruder Krüger to trust me? In order to effectively work with members, we need to earn their trust. I learned from my mistake that I need to be serious when I make a promise and that I need to do what I say I'll do. That is how I could gain the trust of the members.

Members are invaluable in missionary work. They can invite their friends, be friends with new converts, help teach friends, and support friends of the Church and missionaries. We full-time missionaries need to gain their trust, which is what I was not doing when I failed to keep my word and didn't prioritize developing relationships with the soccer-playing members. Trust is essential because members need to trust the missionaries before they help them in the work, give them referrals, or join them in teaching lessons. Learn from my mistakes: Gain the members' trust, and you will have a perfect teammate in the battle to save souls. (Just be careful not to get carried away and side-tackle any old men in your pursuits for trust and unity.)

YOMO Truths: Member Missionary Work

Leaders of the Church are placing great emphasis on member missionary work. Just because you don't have a name tag doesn't mean you aren't a missionary. We are all called to share the gospel in every stage of our lives. The work of gathering Israel, which involves both family history and missionary work, is described by President Nelson as "the greatest challenge, the greatest cause, and the greatest work on earth."[104] With the local leaders in your mission, encourage members to serve alongside you and help gather Israel.

You may be asking, What does member missionary work look like? What can we do as missionaries to better work with members? First, follow the counsel and inspiration of your mission president and leaders. They can guide you on how to work with members and what activities are appropriate, such as holding street displays together, going on joint teaches, and asking them for referrals. Second, the local leaders of your area will likely have missionary goals for their members. Help motivate and inspire members to strive for these goals alongside you. Third, get to know the members and build connections with them as you serve and meet together. My companions and I got to know the members better by teaching small lessons to them in their homes, participating in service activities with them, and inviting them to join us during street displays and lessons. There are lots of ways you can involve the members in missionary work. Be creative and seek inspiration from the Spirit!

Don't underestimate the power of member missionary work. Members truly are your greatest ally in the work of salvation. In the *Liahona* article "The Power of Members and Missionaries Working Together," the author talked about how members can act as a powerful third witness to missionaries' teaching, serving in invaluable ways: "Members can help find, teach, and assist in the conversion process

---

104. Russell M. Nelson, quoted in Charlotte Larcabal, "A Call to Enlist and Gather Israel," *New Era*, Mar. 2019.

of many of the Lord's children that the missionaries would otherwise be unable to or that would take them a long time to accomplish."[105]

Members can share their testimonies and faith with friends of the Church, and they can help find and inspire friends of the Church as well. On my mission, I was grateful for the support of the faithful disciples in Germany. In Lübeck, when my companion and I were teaching a young woman, the bishop joined us for our lesson on tithing. It turned out to be crucial that he was there, as his testimony and knowledge helped our friend gain more faith in Christ and the principle of tithing.

So your next question may be, What can I do to work well with members? From my own mistakes, I can tell you that being trustworthy and reliable is essential to building positive relationships with members. You can build trust by getting to know the members, showing Christlike love, respecting their social norms, and being committed to the work. I wasn't perfect at working with members, but I am grateful for the patience, love, and support they showed me and my fellow missionaries. When we served and taught together, friends of the Church were blessed, and the work progressed. We felt happy and YOMOed!

Additional Mistakes to Avoid and Stories to Enjoy

Here are a couple of pro tips from other mistakes I made with members:

- **Don't be late to appointments with members.** In Germany, punctuality is extremely important. For some reason, I never managed to nail this expectation down. I was always running around like the rabbit in *Alice in Wonderland*, screaming, "I'm late! I'm late! For a very important date!"[106] This caused me to offend and inconvenience some people. Don't make the same mistake—strive to be on time for all meetings and show the members that you value their time and help.

---

105. David W. Adjavon, "The Power of Members and Missionaries Working Together," *Liahona*, July 2018.
106. "The Most Quotable Sayings From *Alice in Wonderland*," Disney News, Apr. 3, 2018, https://news.disney.com/alice-in-wonderland-quotes.

- **Understand and respect their culture.** Learn what the people you serve value. For example, keeping your word and being on time matters a lot in Germany. Learn about and seek to understand the culture of the people you serve and respect their values and traditions.

Here are a couple of stories to enjoy as well:

- **Caroling and candy.** In December, the missionaries in my district and a few members in the area met and sang Christmas songs in the street. Light snow was falling, and small groups of people were beginning to congregate around us. One member suggested that I help pass out candy to the children listening with their parents as a way to strike up more conversations with people. I'm not a big singer, so I was excited to not have to sing, but I was also nervous because I was shy and not sure how to approach people. This ward member kindly took me under his wing and showed me how to pass out the candy to the children and greet the parents. Thanks to this member's instruction, I was able to talk with more people. We can learn so much from the members, and they can encourage us in the work!

- **Street displays.** I loved street displays, and it was exciting and motivating to be spreading the gospel message with others working alongside me. It was humbling to receive support from the members and have them occasionally ask us for advice too. During one winter street display, a member saw me without a scarf and bought me a scarf then and there. Another sister and I would bond over the work and share our experiences of talking to different people. It was fun, and their service made such a difference!

I really enjoyed working with members. I learned so much from them about faith and charity, and when they participated in the work, it was a joyful experience. I have many fond memories of serving with and learning from them during lessons at church, street displays, and youth activities. The members helped me to become a better missionary. Sisters, I promise that as you involve the members in missionary work and serve alongside them, you will YOMO!

YOMO Activity: Help Your Local Missionaries!

I invite you to do an activity with your local missionaries. You could teach a lesson with them, do a service project with them, invite them to dinner, or pray for them. You can learn more about missionary life and participate in this aspect of the work of salvation today!

Study Session: Member Missionary Work

- David W. Adjavon, "The Power of Members and Missionaries Working Together," *Liahona*, July 2018. See also 2 Corinthians 13:1.

- James B. Martino, "Members and Missionaries Working Together," *Ensign*, June 2020. See also the story of Alma and Amulek in Alma 8–16.

- Gordon B. Hinckley, "Words of the Prophet: Reach Out," *New Era*, Feb. 2003. See also Moroni 6:4.

13

Always Strive to Follow the Spirit

The Spirit will guide you in every aspect of the work.

"And a portion of that Spirit dwelleth in me, which giveth me knowledge, and also power according to my faith and desires which are in God." —Alma 18:35

The Spirit and Finding

A couple of weeks before Easter, my mission president issued us a special challenge. He designated April 1st as a "Harvest Day" and asked us to fast to find someone new to teach and then go out and find people to share the gospel with. While I didn't always act on every challenge (and fasting was hard for me!), I acted on this one in a spirit of hope.

On Harvest Day, my companion and I were on our way to a friend of the Church in a cute neighborhood far from the city center of Lübeck. As we walked amid the neatly stacked houses and grassy lawns, basking in the beaming warmth of the sun, I suddenly felt like we should go up to a certain door. But I hesitated. I thought to myself, "We aren't finding right now! We're on our way to our contact, and my companion said nothing about stopping and finding. Is this even a real prompting?" I was about to not say anything since I wasn't sure if it was from the Spirit or just myself. But then I remembered what a Church leader had said about promptings: If you don't know whether it's the Spirit or your thoughts, but it's a good thing, then just do it.

After a ten-minute break with my companion, I summoned up my courage and said, "I have a feeling we need to stop and go back to those rows of houses." We walked back to the houses and knocked on the first door, and a couple invited us in!

"Hello, please come in," the woman said as her husband nodded behind her. The gentleman had a sparkle in his eyes that revealed his love for life. He was energetic and friendly despite his old age. His wife was equally kind and welcoming. They ushered us to the parlor, and we learned that they were Armenian immigrants. They did not speak much German, but they knew Russian and Armenian, so we called an elder who knew a little Russian and had him talk to the gentleman, Herr (Mr.) Aslanyan. (Hopefully they discussed the gospel, but I couldn't understand a word!) While Herr Aslanyan was on the phone, we chatted with his wife, Frau (Mrs.) Aslanyan, in broken German, as she offered us delicious strawberry cake. We learned that they were Christian.

Before we left, Herr and Frau Aslanyan played Armenian music for us and gave us a watercolor painting of Venice! Their charity and love for life touched me. My companion and I decided that we would return the following week with a copy of the Book of Mormon for the couple. In my email home to my family, I wrote about being grateful that I had acted on the prompting to knock on their door. "I just wanted to tell you this story because usually I don't follow those little promptings, but this time I did. I hope I can continue to improve and do it more." In my tender mercies journal, I wrote, "Thank you, inspiration from the Spirit."

We met with Herr and Frau Aslanyan several more times. We received more gorgeous watercolor paintings and gave them the Book of Mormon. They attended church with us, and some elders who spoke Armenian helped teach them the lessons. I don't know if they got baptized, but they were a light to me in Lübeck with their faith, charity, and generosity.

I learned from this experience how important it is to follow promptings from the Spirit despite doubt, fear, and inconvenience (though this is definitely easier to write than to put into practice). I was tempted to ignore the prompting to knock on the Armenian couple's door because I had doubts. I had received a lot of rejection and didn't believe someone would answer, much less be willing to talk to us. I also doubted if the prompting was *real*. Was it from the Spirit or just from me? However, I'm glad that I acted on the wise advice from a Church leader that you'll never regret acting on a positive impression, whether it's from your own intuition or from God. This time, acting on inspiration led to being able to teach a couple!

Fear can also be a *huge* hindrance to acting on spiritual promptings. Often, I feared people's reactions. My main concern was offending people. Would they get upset if I gave them a copy of the Book of Mormon? Invited them to Church? I let fear get the best of me too many times. So my suggestion for overcoming fear and acting on promptings is just to keep trying and practicing. Practice makes perfect (or nearly perfect). The more you manage to follow promptings, the easier it gets. Another piece of advice is to focus more on your righteous goals and desires instead of worrying about negative outcomes. As the *Come Follow Me* 2024 manual explains, this is what the sons of Mosiah did in the Book of Mormon. They were Nephites, and they went to preach to the Lamanites, who were their enemies and were not followers of God. Instead of focusing on fear and rejection, the sons of Mosiah "had an even stronger reason why they felt they must share the gospel with the Lamanites": They had experienced the Savior's love and redemption, and they wanted every soul to be saved.[107] Think about your "stronger reason" when sharing the gospel.

Honestly, the final and most significant obstacle for me that day was inconvenience. We had an appointment, and ringing doorbells wasn't my favorite activity. Also, I regarded my companion as more of the leader in our companionship, so it felt challenging to speak up

---

107. "July 1–7: 'I Will Make an Instrument of Thee' | Alma 17–22," *Come, Follow Me—For Home and Church: Book of Mormon 2024*.

and lead for once. But thankfully, after hesitating, I did speak up, and we met a remarkable couple. Overcoming obstacles such as doubt, fear, and inconvenience can be difficult, but as you strive to follow the Spirit's promptings, you'll receive blessings, and your ability to heed the Holy Ghost will be strengthened. This is Heavenly Father's work. He wants you to succeed and will not leave you without a guide. The Spirit will help you in your pursuits to find people to teach and baptize.

The Spirit and Teaching

On a beautiful spring day with vibrant flowers in full bloom, my companion and I went to teach Sister Wisniewski, a recent convert in Lübeck. (I loved teaching lessons to new converts because of their energy and enthusiasm for the gospel of Christ.) Sister Wisniewski was a kind Polish woman with short hair and glasses whose eyes lit up when she shared her love for Christ and His gospel. After visiting her weekly for a couple of months, I built a friendship with her and loved seeing her progress in her knowledge and faith.

On this particular day, I had a whole lesson planned out that I was excited to teach. My companion and I greeted Sister Wisniewski and sat down at her kitchen table across from her. Then, as I was about to open my mouth and begin the lesson, I felt a strong impression from the Spirit that I should change what we had planned and testify about temples instead. Being too stubborn, I initially resisted the prompting, thinking to myself, "No, I really want to teach the lesson we planned." But the Spirit became too strong, so I yielded and said to Sister Wisniewski, "Today, we're going to talk about temples." My companion went along with it, and we testified of temples and their crucial role in God's plan and our lives.

At the end of the lesson, Sister Wisniewski cried. She said, "I feel the Spirit strongly." I was glad I had ditched our plans and followed the Spirit!

Heavenly Father knows us perfectly, and He knew that Sister Wisniewski needed to learn about temples that day. I am embarrassed that I resisted the prompting initially but grateful that I eventually listened. The Spirit is never wrong! Follow the Spirit's promptings when teaching. As the Savior taught in Matthew 10:19–20, "Take no thought how or what ye shall speak: for it shall be given you in that same hour what ye shall speak." Study diligently, be prepared, and seek the Holy Ghost's direction when planning and teaching lessons. Teach with the Spirit, and you will touch people's hearts.

YOMO Truths: Finding, Teaching, and Serving with the Spirit

Honestly, you can launch this book across the room, ignore all my advice, and still have a very successful, happy mission by doing one thing: seeking and following the promptings of the Spirit. Listening to the Holy Ghost is the number one thing you can do to have a YOMO mission. The Spirit is essential to the work. As Elder Bednar taught, "The Holy Ghost is the third member of the Godhead, and He is the witness of all truth and the ultimate and true teacher. . . . We should become and remain worthy conduits through whom the Spirit of the Lord can operate. . . . We must be careful to remember in our service that we are conduits and channels; we are not the light."[108]

I want to add an important point from Elder Uchtdorf: that we don't convert people—the Spirit does.[109] This is significant! It's the Holy Ghost who "reveals and teaches 'the truth of all things.'"[110] We are merely the instruments through which the Spirit can pass, as Elder Bednar described.

Elder Bednar also taught that "our best efforts can only bring the message of truth *unto* the heart (see 2 Nephi 33:1). Ultimately, a friend of the Church needs to act in righteousness and thereby invite the truth *into* his or her own heart."[111] We need to remember that our friends of the Church have a role in gospel learning and can choose to accept the message or not. It can be frustrating when they decide not to let the Spirit in or don't accept our sincere invitations to act and

---

108. David A. Bednar, "Becoming a Preach My Gospel Missionary," from a devotional address given at the Provo Missionary Training Center on June 24, 2011, ChurchofJesusChrist.org.
109. Dieter F. Uchtdorf, "Missionary Work: Sharing What Is in Your Heart," *Ensign* or *Liahona*, May 2019, 17.
110. Topics and Questions, "Holy Ghost," Gospel Library.
111. David A. Bednar, "Becoming a Preach My Gospel Missionary."

learn more. However, we can try not to become discouraged while allowing everyone their agency and showing love for people. This isn't always easy, but it's more important to invite and love than to invite and judge.

In addition, Elder Bednar said that because friends of the Church must invite the truth into their hearts, we as missionaries need to not only "learn to teach by the power of the Spirit" but also "help investigators learn by faith and by the power of the Holy Ghost."[112] I like how Elder Bednar used the word *learn*. It takes time to learn how to teach with the Holy Ghost and to teach others to learn with the Holy Ghost. We can start by showing friends of the Church how to study the scriptures, apply the principles to their lives, and sincerely pray to God, their Heavenly Father, who wants to provide them with direction and help.

As you strive to teach with the Holy Ghost, I invite you sisters to utilize the gifts of the Spirit. These gifts can include many talents and abilities, from knowledge to healing to understanding foreign languages (see Doctrine and Covenants 46). They will enhance your capacity to serve, lead, and testify.

You may be wondering, How do we learn to recognize and follow the Spirit as we find and teach people? First, know that learning to recognize and heed the promptings of the Holy Ghost is a lifelong process! You won't master it entirely in one day, but you can start now, before your mission, to learn how the Spirit speaks to you. For example, I have gradually learned that I am most in tune with the Holy Ghost when I'm in nature or sincerely studying the scriptures.

As you learn more about revelation from the Spirit, it's important to note that revelation comes in different ways, including on your mission. One day, you may feel a very strong prompting to go to a certain street or teach a specific gospel topic. On another day, you may feel a quiet, warm feeling in your heart as you do your best to serve. In his talk "The Spirit of Revelation," Elder Bednar compared strong versus subtle promptings to different ways we experience light. He explained that revelations can be grand and instantaneous, like a light entering a dark room; however, more often, they are quieter and more

---

112. David A. Bednar, "Becoming a Preach My Gospel Missionary."

incremental, like a sunrise.[113] Personally, I've experienced more of the latter. I've had moments when I felt the Spirit strongly and I knew exactly what the Holy Ghost wanted me to do and say, but more often, I've simply felt the Spirit's peaceful presence. It's easy to expect something bigger and miss the sunrises God sends us. However, I know that these sunrises of revelation bring hope, joy, light, and peace.

On days you feel less inspired, feed your soul with His word and rejuvenate your spirit by doing a small activity that will bring you peace and joy, such as taking a walk in a park or reviewing God's promises to you in your patriarchal blessing. For me, I felt more distanced from the Spirit when I was only focused on my troubles or when I doubted my worth or purpose. Sisters, please don't doubt your everlasting worth as daughters of God! You have been endowed with power to accomplish the Lord's purposes.

The final piece of advice on this topic I'd like to share is from Ammon's story in the Book of Mormon. On his mission, Ammon explained to King Lamoni that the Spirit called him to preach to him and his people and that "a portion of that Spirit dwelleth in me, which giveth me knowledge, and also power according to my faith and desires which are in God" (Alma 18:35).

I love this verse! We have access to that same power that Ammon had as a missionary—the Holy Ghost. We too have been called by the Spirit to teach Christ's gospel to our brothers and sisters. While we probably won't be chopping off arms to protect sheep like Ammon did (see Alma 17:37), the Spirit can give us "knowledge" and "power" as we have faith and righteous desires. The Holy Ghost will empower you to do the Lord's work.

Additional Tips on Finding and Teaching with the Holy Ghost:

1. Obedience and unity with your companion are very important parts of teaching with the Spirit. Strive to have a positive relationship with your companion. (There are more tips on this in the next chapter.)

---

113. David A. Bednar, "The Spirit of Revelation," *Ensign* or *Liahona*, May 2011, 87.

2. Do your homework before teaching! The Spirit can help you recall information to share in a lesson (see John 14:26), but you need to give the Spirit something to help you recall first. Study the lessons in *Preach My Gospel*, ponder the scriptures, and strengthen your testimony, and then the Spirit will help you know what to share and when.

3. Be sensitive to the needs of the people you teach and follow the impressions you receive from the Spirit, even if it means changing up your lesson game plan. Trust that God knows what people need to hear! It's a blessing to be guided by the Spirit, and it's the most effective way to teach.

4. With finding, keep in mind that both you and your companion can receive promptings from the Spirit. Whether a prompting comes to you or your companion, act in unity and follow inspiration together.

5. Regarding finding, you can pray for the Spirit's help and comfort. When I struggled, I found it helpful to pray for the comfort and peace that only the Holy Ghost can bring (see John 14:27).

YOMO Activity: Learn About Revelation

Watch Elder Bednar's video "Patterns of Light: Spiritual Revelation."[114] Then discuss the following questions with a friend or parent:

1. How does Elder Bednar describe revelation?
2. Why is one of the Savior's names "the Light"?
3. What can you do to increase your spiritual capacity to receive revelation, as President Nelson has instructed us to do?[115]

---

114. David A. Bednar, "Patterns of Light: Spirit of Revelation" (video), Gospel Library.
115. Russell M. Nelson, "Revelation for the Church, Revelation for Our Lives," *Ensign* or *Liahona*, May 2018, 93–96.

Study Session: Following the Promptings of the Holy Ghost

- David A. Bednar, "Becoming a Preach My Gospel Missionary," from a devotional address given at the Provo Missionary Training Center on June 24, 2011, ChurchofJesusChrist.org.
- David A. Bednar, "Patterns of Light: Spiritual Revelation" (video), Gospel Library.
- David A. Bednar, "The Spirit of Revelation," *Ensign* or *Liahona*, May 2011, 87–90.
- Jane H. Lassetter, "'Lead Me, Guide Me, Walk Beside Me': Life Lessons with the Holy Ghost" (Brigham Young University devotional, Mar. 4, 2014), speeches.byu.edu.
- Gospel Topics, "Holy Ghost," Gospel Library.
- Chapters 4 ("Seek and Rely on the Spirit") and 10 ("Teach to Build Faith in Christ"), *Preach My Gospel: A Guide to Sharing the Gospel of Jesus Christ* (2023).
- Alma 18:35; 2 Nephi 32:1–5; Doctrine and Covenants 8:2–3; Luke 12:12

14

All about Companions

*Getting along with companions isn't easy!
But there's power in sisterhood.*

"Learning patience and love, practicing forgiveness, and accepting differences in personalities will bless you throughout your life."[116]

A Short Sister Saga

Before becoming a missionary, I prided myself on *always* getting along with other young women. I never got into drama. I never went after a guy another girl liked (I also never thought I could actually get the guy, but that's a different story). I thought I was a loyal and fun friend. Then I went on my mission and started living with companions, other young women, for seven days a week and twenty-four hours a day. It was a lot! A big life adjustment. Early on in my mission, I started noticing how I would get irritated with my companions and seemingly annoy them in return. We had disagreements and some

---

116. "2.2.1: Supporting Each Other," in "Missionary Organization and Activities," *Missionary Standards for Disciples of Jesus Christ*, ChurchofJesusChrist.org.

awkward moments. I thought to myself, "This isn't me! I've always been good at getting along with girls—what's wrong with me now?" Let me tell you, it's normal to have conflicts with companions. It's normal to struggle with a companion you most likely did not know beforehand and did not choose to be with and who may be very different from you. However, while companionships can be challenging, they can also be fun and rewarding.

In a city in the eastern state of Sachsen, I served with Sister Cho. I had been serving in the area for one transfer before she arrived as my new companion. Sister Cho had fashionable clothing and wore her short, dark hair in a pretty bob. She was warm, outgoing, and a gifted violinist. She was also the only sister from South Korea in the Berlin mission. (Most of the sisters were American.) She had the challenge of navigating both English and German as non-native languages, which she did remarkably well.

During our first week together, things got off to a rough start when I failed to properly direct us to the Church building for our district meeting (our weekly meeting with the other missionaries serving in the same area). The German train and bus system is amazing, but I was, and still am, terrible at directions! Thankfully, I soon found out that one of Sister Cho's talents was reading maps and navigating us to our destinations. I think it was Sister Cho who got us to the church that day, even though it was her first day going there.

After that district meeting, our next couple of months were a bit of an adjustment. I was learning how to be the leader of an area for once, and I made many mistakes, including in navigation. There were also cultural differences to learn about and get used to. Sometime during those initial sweltering summer months, Sister Cho and I went to McDonald's. We were both craving those greasy fries and refreshing shakes! After we ordered our food and sat down at a white table near the window, Sister Cho began eating my fries.

Since I am extremely passionate and possessive about food, I inwardly started freaking out: "No one touches my fries! Why is she eating my fries? I do *not* share my food, not ever, and definitely not something as precious as delicious fries!" I stayed calm on the outside, however. Sister Cho began eating her food, and I started chomping down on my wrap when she asked, "Do you want some of my food?

Here, try my nuggets," and then she slid the container over to me. Surprised, I said, "Sure," and ate a couple of McNuggets.

A few weeks later, Sister Cho and I made a deal that she'd cook for us and I'd do the dishes (the best deal I ever made on my mission since she made such delicious food). I noticed that when arranging meals, Sister Cho would place all the pots in the middle, and then she would have us take from each pot and put the food on our plates. It finally dawned on me that sharing food was a part of her culture, a South Korean custom. In my American (and personally selfish) mindset, I had been confused by how she took and offered food, but once I understood it was part of her culture, we had unity at mealtimes. (And we had plates full of flavor: Sister Cho prepared healthy meat and rice dishes, perfectly seasoned veggies, and beautiful fried zucchini. I miss it!)

As warm summer evenings slipped into chilly autumn mornings, Sister Cho and I faced a lot of obstacles together. A friend of the Church ghosted us after we gave her a tour of the Freiberg temple. We didn't have many people to teach, and we faced lots of rejection during street contacting. She and I learned to help one another during these and various personal challenges, and our relationship became stronger.

However, after our second transfer together, we both hoped for a change. We expected to be transferred to a new area, and we were so certain that we wouldn't be companions anymore that we decorated each other's Tschüss Bücher (goodbye books) with pictures and memories. However, when we got our transfer call in early September, the office elders told us, "Both you and Sister Cho will be staying together in [the Sachsen city] for another six weeks."

We were devastated at the news. We had experienced hard times in our area and had already been together for two transfers. However, Heavenly Father had a different plan for us, and He wanted us to serve together for another month and a half.

With help from the Spirit, that last transfer with Sister Cho turned out to be positive. Having few people to teach was still difficult, but Sister Cho and I grew even closer. The Holy Ghost helped me become less selfish and filled my heart with charity for my companion and others. Sister Cho and I had a lot of fun together too.

For one of our final preparation days, we took a train to a nearby castle. Since it was a Monday (and many public places in Germany aren't open then), the castle was closed, but we got to explore the stunning grounds. Rows of trees had just transitioned from rich greens to vibrant yellows and reds, and water fountains greeted us around every corner of the castle's maze-like gardens. In a private corner surrounded by trees, I offered a prayer as requested by Sister Cho. It was a special bonding moment. The beauty and peace of nature enveloped us as we overlooked the forested German countryside together. It was like a scene from a dream, and I loved it. Sister Cho really seemed to enjoy it as well.

That day at the castle and throughout our last transfer together, Sister Cho and I were able to YOMO more. Most importantly, we gradually learned how to better YOMO together as a united companionship. Things started out hard, but when that third transfer ended, we were best friends. She helped me a lot along the way, and I hope I also helped her. We had a lot of adventures and laughs together. She became one of my closest friends on the mission, and whenever I ran into her at a meeting or a train station, we greeted each other with excitement. One day, she called me to update me on friends from our area, and in my tender mercies journal, I wrote, "Sister Cho called! Ah! It was really fun to talk to her! So fun to hear her voice!"

Throughout my mission, I had many highs and lows with companions. Some companions became my best friends, like Sister Cho. I also became close to sisters in my districts and zones. Other companions were more challenging for me. I sometimes fell into the trap (and still do) of focusing too much on the drama and flaws in my relationships when, instead, I needed to highlight the strengths of my friendships more.

On your mission, you will encounter obstacles in companionships, but remember that the sisters you serve with have the potential to be your greatest allies and cheerleaders in the mission field (and even outside the mission field too as friends and roommates). You can relate to and help one another as you face similar challenges. Befriend your companions and other sisters in the mission. Not only will it positively impact the work, but you can make a lot of fun memories together that you will cherish forever.

In my tender mercies journal on June 29, 2017, two months before the end of my mission, I wrote, "Zone conference in Freiberg was spiritual and fun. I felt the Spirit throughout most of the meeting and felt love and unity with the other sisters—I love 'em all, and we've had nearly a mission of memories together." Embrace your sister power and strive for unity. Then you'll be unstoppable!

YOMO Truths: Serving in Unity with Companions

Being unified with your companion is essential to the work *and* your personal happiness. It's not always easy, but it's worth the effort and will help you YOMO! So I'd like to share with you more about the "why" and "how" of serving with companions.

In the *Liahona* article "Adjusting to Life as a Missionary: Companions, Rejection, and Mental Health," author Holly Hudson referenced three scriptures that help explain the "why" of missionary companions.[117] First, missionaries need companions because it's the Lord's established pattern. Doctrine and Covenants 42:6 reads, "And ye shall go forth in the power of my Spirit, preaching my gospel, two by two, in my name, lifting up your voices as with the sound of a trump, declaring my word like unto angels of God." Second, it's important that we teach in pairs because companions offer a second witness of gospel truth. Hudson gave the example of when Amulek confirmed Alma's words with his testimony when the pair preached to the people of Ammonihah (see Alma 10).

Her third scripture illustrates another reason for companionships: You can strengthen and help one another, as Alma attended to Amulek after their missionary service. Alma 15:18 reads, "Now as I said, Alma having seen all these things, therefore he took Amulek and came over to the land of Zarahemla, and took him to his own house, and did administer unto him in his tribulations, and strengthened him in the Lord."

As companions, you have a responsibility and opportunity to help each other during times of trial and to nurture each other in the gospel of Christ. Building unity in your companionship is important

---

117. Holly Hudson, "Adjusting to Life as a Missionary: Companions, Rejection, and Mental Health," *Liahona*, Feb. 2021.

because unity blesses the work, bringing you and your fellow sister increased happiness and peace.

Now, I want to make a disclaimer: I wasn't the best companion and often didn't even think about being a good one. It was challenging being with someone 24/7. However, I know that we can pray to our Heavenly Father about our concerns with any aspect of the work, including problems with our companions, and the Spirit can help us become a better companion as well.

Don't demand perfection of yourself or your companion—just strive to improve. Also, don't forget that having a companion can be fun! Not every moment will be a challenge. You'll get to know each other, laugh together, and have epic adventures, and when challenges come, you can support and comfort one another. You don't have to go through hard times alone. With every companion, you can learn vital life lessons. You can grow as a daughter and as a disciple of the Lord.

YOMO Tips on Companionships from an Imperfect Sister:

Here's a list of tips from me, a missionary who sometimes struggled with companions but who learned a lot of valuable lessons along the way.

1. **Remember you can learn something new from every sister you serve with.** While I was with my first trainer, I learned how to be positive and energetic about the work and serve with all my heart, might, mind, and strength. (She was definitely a YOMO missionary!) From another companion, I developed more patience and empathy. In a word, this is what I learned from each of my eleven companions: passion, diligence, self-awareness, connection, service, self-improvement, self-worth, commitment, grace, charity, and forgiveness. While you will have different experiences with different companions, everyone has something to teach you, either through their words or their example. Seek to be open-minded and learn from each of your companions.

2. **Do your best.** You will have a variety of companions. Some companions may be younger than you, some older. Some may

be more introverted or more extroverted than you. Some you may get along with naturally, while others you may struggle to "click" with. As my dad said in his letter to me, "Some of your companions you will love and others you will tolerate. Just do your best." The key point here is to "do your best." Strive to get to know all your companions and serve them.

3. **Seek the Spirit's help.** No matter what challenges you may face in your companionships, know that the Holy Ghost can help you. Pray for charity and follow the promptings you receive to serve your companion, and your relationship will be strengthened.

4. **Be a good companion yourself.** I'm going to be honest: If I wanted my relationship to improve, my first reaction was wishing my companion would change! However, I'm gradually learning how essential it is to serve and take charge of what we can control. Strive to be a kind and caring friend to your companion. Likely, your positivity will rub off on her, and you'll have a happier relationship.

5. **Communicate!** When you get a new companion, talk to her and learn her story. Getting to know my companions helped me understand them and become closer friends with them. In addition, when problems arise, don't let them fester. Communicate kindly to your companion about what's bothering you. Strive to give her the benefit of the doubt, seek to understand her perspective when you address issues, and always apologize. Be honest with one another, and strive to have charity for each other.

6. **Help your companion first.** This was something that took me too long to realize, but your companion is just as important as the people you teach. Prioritize your companion and their needs. If they're struggling, help them like you would a friend of the Church. Support them in their trials, and help them strengthen their faith. Mosiah 18:8–9 teaches us to be true disciples and to "mourn with those that mourn" and "comfort

those that stand in need of comfort." Bear each other's burdens. Comfort your companion and be there for her.

7. **Remember that you only have control over yourself.** It's important to remember that everyone has agency, including your companions. They may choose at times not to communicate or try to repair things. In these cases, remember that you only have control over your actions. Don't place pressure on yourself or on her for the companionship to be perfect. Just do your best and continue striving to be the companion you'd like to be. Seek help from trusted leaders within the mission when there are unresolved issues.

YOMO Activity: Spread Light

Pray and ask God who you could reach out to this week. If a name comes to your mind, reach out to that person and serve them in some small way. Reflect on your experience.

Study Session: All About Companions

- Jose L. Alonso, "Love One Another as He Has Loved Us," *Ensign* or *Liahona*, Nov. 2017, 119–21.

- *The Errand of Angels*, directed by Christian Vuissa (Excel Entertainment Group, 2008). This is a movie about a sister missionary serving in Austria.

- Rebecca Mills Hume and Brad Wilcox, "From Friends to Sisters to Companions," *New Era*, Mar. 2007, 12–13.

- Holly Hudson, "Adjusting to Life as a Missionary: Companions, Rejections, and Mental Health," *Liahona*, Feb. 2021.

- 1 Nephi 3:7; Mosiah 2:17; Mosiah 18:8–9; Moroni 7:46–48

15

Sources of Support

This isn't a season of *Survivor*.
You won't be expected to face any solo challenges.

"Now they never had fought, yet they did not fear death; and they did think more upon the liberty of their fathers than they did upon their lives; yea, they had been taught by their mothers, that if they did not doubt, God would deliver them. And they rehearsed unto me the words of their mothers, saying: We do not doubt our mothers knew it." —Alma 56:47–48

Senior Missionaries Are Amazing!

Sisters, multiple sources of support are available to you as you serve. On my mission, one of my favorite sources of support was senior missionaries. They are literally the best! As you serve alongside senior missionaries, I invite you to learn from their examples of faith, love, and wisdom. They provide essential service in the work of salvation. I'd like to share a story about one senior couple that blessed my life and mission.

I met the Schmidts as I served alongside them during my first transfer in a small, beautiful town in Sachsen. Brother Schmidt was from Germany and was cheerful and energetic. Sister Schmidt was American and conveyed Christlike love through her kind eyes and bright smile. Any time our district met, Brother and Sister Schmidt were always there, participating and helping lead and guide us younger missionaries. They helped a lot with service projects and anything related to the temple. As a brand-new missionary in the area, I found their faith and grandparent-like love extremely comforting. They greeted me and everyone else with beaming smiles and had genuine conversations with anyone who crossed their paths.

One of my favorite memories with this sweet couple, when their love for others was on full display, was on a spring day when they invited my companion and me to go on a bike ride. We had been inside all day, doing a mission-wide Book of Mormon challenge, and while I had enjoyed reading the scriptures, I was itching to go outside. I was delighted by the invitation from Brother and Sister Schmidt and grateful for a little break and some fresh air.

We drove with the Schmidts to a nearby trail and unloaded the bikes from the car. We got onto the path, which led to a forest. Brother Schmidt called it "a Red Riding Hood forest," and I couldn't agree more. As we pedaled into the woods, I smiled with delight and peered up at the thick canopy above me. The trees were tall and dark, with green pine needles and vibrant leaves piercing the sky. As we cruised through the forest, I held my face to the fresh breeze and felt extreme gratitude for this moment of exercise and fairytale fun.

After biking for a few glorious miles, we stopped at a quaint café nestled among the trees that Sister Schmidt said "only the locals go to." It had a brown roof, white walls, and the most flavorful, delicious Bratwurst I have ever tasted. After savoring each bite of sausage, we all biked back toward our car, at one point encountering a group of young German men who clearly had been drinking and partying but now were just chilling. Brother Schmidt said hello to them and showed them the same Christlike love he and Sister Schmidt showered on everyone. He did not judge the young men for drinking or having other standards.

That moment in the woods impressed me. Brother and Sister Schmidt truly practiced what they preached. They brightened the lives of everyone they met, including mine, and made my mission extra joyful.

In addition, they supported my companion and me spiritually and gave us ideas on how to help the people we were teaching. Above all, it was their charity, their Christlike love for all of God's children, that impressed me the most. They taught me that true disciples of Christ strive to love as He did. As the Savior counseled His Apostles, "By this shall all men know that ye are my disciples, if ye have love one to another" (John 13:35).

I am so grateful for the Schmidts and for all the senior missionaries I had the pleasure of serving with in Germany. Sisters, let the senior missionaries out there know that their service matters. They are an important source of strength to us in the mission field! About senior missionaries, President Nelson said, "Seniors strengthen the younger elders and sisters. They provide support that helps others to serve better in their own responsibilities. . . . Senior couples are often a literal answer to the prayers of bishops and branch presidents."[118]

Senior couples, you matter! Sisters, if you have the opportunity to work with senior missionaries, enjoy your time with them. Serving in unity will bring joy and many YOMO memories!

In addition to senior missionaries, there are other sources of support in the mission field, including, but not limited to, the mission president and his wife, sister training leaders, and local Church leaders and members. For example, my sister training leaders (female missionaries assigned to care for and help lead sisters within their area) gave me helpful advice regarding my companionships, and they lifted my spirits by baking me cookies and listening to me talk about my experiences and struggles. Under the authority of the bishop, ward mission leaders directed the work and guided us missionaries on how to best serve the ward. Relief Society sisters taught lessons with us and encouraged us. They checked on us and ensured we had what we needed to serve effectively. Sisters, you will not be left alone. Many valiant members and leaders will join you in the work of salvation.

---

118. Russell M. Nelson, "Senior Missionary Moments," *Ensign*, Apr. 2016, 67.

Dear Parents and Trusted Mentors, We Need You!

Being on a mission, away from home for eighteen months, made me really appreciate my family. My parents were and still are a vital source of support and strength in my life. If you can, take opportunities to learn from your parents. Be present when they share their testimonies or teach you about a gospel message. Appreciate their examples of faith. If they served missions, ask them about their experiences and what advice they have for you. If you lack a spiritual leader in your home, you can reach out to trusted mentors and ask them for guidance and help. Sometimes older people actually *are* wiser! We can learn from the life experience and advice of those who have traveled through life's different stages before us.

When you're on your mission, you can continue to seek advice from your parents or mentors back home. I had a mindset of "I have to figure this out on my own and be an adult," so I didn't tell my loved ones about any of my challenges during the mission. (I told them about it afterward, though, which honestly was therapeutic but not as helpful.) While we as young adults need to become independent and make decisions on our own, we still need help sometimes, and it's okay to ask for it. Your parents likely know you better than anyone else, so they may be able to give you some of the best advice and support.

YOMO Tips to Include Families in Missionary Work

Here are a few ways your family can get involved in the work:

- They can write their testimonies in a copy of the Book of Mormon and send it to you. (You can translate their testimonies first if needed.) Give that copy of the Book of Mormon to a friend of the Church.

- They can pray for you and for the people you're teaching.

- They can pray as a family to find someone they can share the gospel of Christ with.

- They can help support the missionaries in their ward and teach lessons with them. Then they can share their experiences with you.

- They can send inspirational quotes and scriptures to you along with letters and homemade cards. They can express their love for and trust in you.

- They can invite members in their ward to send encouraging emails to you.

- Seek the Spirit's inspiration as a family and come up with your own ideas!

Youth Leaders Are Awesome!

While preparing to write this book, I read through my old missionary emails and came across shout-outs to my youth leaders. On September 27, 2016, I wrote to my family, "Those times I felt the Spirit at girls' camp and those opportunities to feel the Spirit [in lessons and at activities] strengthened my testimony, and I will have them forever to help me in my life."

Take advantage of the youth program! My testimony was strengthened in my teenage years by the faithful examples of my youth leaders, their love and care, and their activities that gave me opportunities to feel the Holy Ghost. In an email, I wrote, "If I could tell the young women anything, I would tell them to take the time to develop a desire to gain a testimony and then study, learn, and serve." The time to build your testimony is now! Take charge of your gospel learning. Build friendships with other young women and have fun too! Continue enjoying activities, developing meaningful relationships, and growing spiritually as a young adult. Additionally, if you recently joined the Church or didn't go through the youth program, know that your experiences and perspectives will be a blessing to your mission.

No matter what stage of life you're in and whether you choose to serve a mission, further develop and nurture your faith. Your testimony matters and can be a great source of strength to you. As President Uchtdorf said, "Some may say that the steps [to receiving a testimony or witness of spiritual truths] are too hard or that they are not worth the effort. But I suggest that this personal testimony of the gospel and the Church is the most important thing you can earn in this life. It will not only bless and guide you during this life, but it will also have a direct bearing on your life throughout eternity."[119]

Sisters, your faith and influence matter. I promise that your testimony will bless your life forever and that the Lord has great things in store for you. Developing your faith will not only help you YOMO, but it'll also help you achieve your divine destiny.

YOMO Activity: Discussion Questions with a Parent, Mentor, or Youth Leader

Ask a parent, mentor, or youth leader the following questions:

1. What helped you strengthen your testimony and build your faith?

2. What does the Savior's Atonement mean to you? How have you felt His love and comfort in your life?

3. How have you felt the Holy Ghost's guidance in your life? What helps you be in tune with the Spirit?

4. If you served a mission, how did the Holy Ghost help you as a missionary?

5. What other advice would you give to me about serving a mission?

Study Session: Sources of Strength

- Robert D. Hales, "The Importance of Receiving a Personal Testimony," *Ensign*, Nov. 1994, 20–22.

- Russell M. Nelson, "Senior Missionary Moments," *Ensign*, Apr. 2016, 66–68.

- "Tahitian Woman and Young Woman Express Thanks for Their Youth Leaders," September 10, 2020, newsroom.ChurchofJesusChrist.org.

---

119. Dieter F. Uchtdorf, "Receiving a Testimony of Light and Truth," *Ensign* or *Liahona*, Nov. 2014, 22.

- Richard M. Romney, "Parents, Help Them to Prepare," *Ensign,* Aug. 2018.
- 1 Timothy 4:12; Alma 56:46–48

16

HOW TO PREPARE PHYSICALLY, MENTALLY, EMOTIONALLY, SPIRITUALLY, AND SOCIALLY

**I *so* wasn't fully prepared for my mission.
You don't have to be perfectly prepared to serve,
but preparation never hurt anyone.**

"Missionaries are most likely to experience success when they are worthy and physically, mentally, and emotionally prepared for missionary service."[120]

This chapter is all about how to prepare for a mission so you can more easily YOMO. I hand-picked tips from my mental folder of "what I wish I had known before I served" to share with you. As you read this chapter, remember that you don't have to be perfectly prepared to serve a mission. No one (besides Jesus) is a perfect missionary. So don't feel like you need to master every item on this list, but consider

---

120. Richard M. Romney, "Parents, Help Them to Prepare," *Ensign*, Aug. 2018, 40.

my advice and follow the Spirit to best prepare for your missionary service. For example, you could focus on one area that stands out to you or work on a couple of goals from different sections. I added tips on how to continue to grow and serve while on your mission as well.

YOMO Tip #1: Know That a Mission Will Be Hard But Worth It

I must tell you this since no one really told me: Missions are so hard! I was frustrated that everyone seemed to only talk about the good stuff, and then I went on a mission and learned that a lot of hard stuff happens, such as soul-stretching personal growth and a strict work schedule. At the beginning of my mission, I felt like someone had promised me a colossal chocolate layered cake with rich icing and lots of sugar, and instead, I got a squishy, measly Brussels sprout. I thought to myself, "This is not what I signed up for! Why did no one warn me how hard it would be?" So this is me informing you that your mission will be difficult. It'll be difficult but worth it.

From my experience, a large part of the reason missions are so challenging is that missionaries typically spend a lot more time in the growth zone than in the comfort zone. If you're anything like me, that may not sound super appealing. I like my comfort zone and try to dodge difficult things if I can help it. However, missions are rewarding because they are challenging. On a mission, you can grow spiritually. You have many opportunities to increase your faith. As you learn more about the gospel of Christ and yourself, face challenges, make mistakes, and learn and improve, you will become a more Christlike disciple. You'll further develop your potential and become who you're meant to be.

Along with trials and growth, there are deep joys and unique opportunities to experience. Sharing the gospel of Christ will give you great happiness. As Elder Ulisses Soares said, "I testify to you that by losing ourselves in the Lord's work, with our eye single to the glory of God, a new light will enter our lives and a renewed joy will fill our hearts. There is no other service in the world that brings more joy in our life than this [missionary work]."[121]

I promise you that serving the Lord will bring you the greatest joy! I felt great joy as I shared my testimony and taught people about the gospel of Christ. Sharing the gospel brought me happiness because the Savior's message brings hope. It's a message about our purpose and how we can find peace and healing. It was amazing to connect with people spiritually and see them as my brothers and sisters. Befriending people from all walks of life was unforgettable and astounding. I still cherish the people from my mission and the adventures, memories, and life lessons.

So yes, your mission will be hard, likely in ways unique to you. However, it'll be worth it. My mission was challenging, but I don't regret serving. It blessed my life in immeasurable ways, and it will also bless your life immeasurably. As Elder Richard G. Scott promises, "While a mission is not for personal advantage, the Lord richly blesses those who valiantly serve."[122] Instead of receiving a colossal chocolate layered cake with rich icing and lots of sugar like I expected, I ended up with a whole buffet of blessings from my mission, including flavorful fruit, delectable cheeses, zesty pasta dishes, and rows of cake.

YOMO Tip #2: Know What "Successful" as a Missionary Means (And What It Doesn't Mean)

What defines a successful missionary? *Preach My Gospel* offers a definition: "Your success as a missionary is determined primarily by your desire and commitment to find, teach, baptize, and confirm converts and to help them become faithful disciples of Christ and members of His Church."[123]

There are a couple of words I'd like to highlight here: *desire* and *commitment*. It's your effort that matters, not your results. It's not about how many people you find, teach, or baptize; it's about your

---

121. Ulisses Soares, quoted in Scott Taylor, "Elder Soares Shares Five Principles for Finding and Using Joy in Missionary Work," *Church News*, July 1, 2019.
122. Richard G. Scott, "Realize Your Full Potential," *Ensign* or *Liahona*, Nov. 2003, 43.
123. *Preach My Gospel: A Guide to Sharing the Gospel of Jesus Christ* (2023), 13.

dedication to the Lord. Don't believe the myth that numbers determine the success of your mission; it's about your willingness to serve.

Preach My Gospel goes on to explain a very important concept, which is that people have agency! You can do everything right as a missionary, and people may still not want to hear your message or choose not to get baptized. Don't take rejection as a personal reflection of yourself as a missionary. As *Preach My Gospel* teaches, "When you have done your best, you may still have disappointments, but you will not be disappointed in yourself. You can feel assured that the Lord is pleased when you feel the Spirit working through you."[124]

You are called to be an instrument in the Lord's hands, remembering that the Lord directs His work, and by feeling the Spirit, people will choose to convert or not.[125] Have faith in God and His plan for you. Don't compare yourself to other missionaries who may appear more "successful" on paper. Use goals to motivate and guide you, but minister to the one, remembering that behind every number is a child of God. You can do much good that cannot be quantified. Strive to meet your goals, prayerfully involving the Lord, and know that your success as a missionary is more about your commitment and effort than about mission statistics.

YOMO Tip #3: Prepare Not Only Spiritually but Physically, Mentally, and Socially Too

Here is something I wish I had known before I served: You need to be more than spiritually prepared to serve a mission! While spiritual preparation is essential, a mission is more than spiritually demanding. It can be physically, mentally, emotionally, and socially demanding as well. So the following section contains suggestions on how you can prepare in each of those areas for your mission.

I invite you to read the following tips with the Spirit in your heart. Don't view this list like a checklist in which you must cross off everything to be ready to serve. Anything you do besides being worthy and willing to serve is extra. Much of this advice is also based on gospel fundamentals, and you are likely doing more than you realize. Keep

---

124. *Preach My Gospel*, 14.
125. See "Seek and Rely on the Spirit," *Preach My Gospel*, 101–111.

in mind President Monson's comforting counsel, "Whom the Lord calls, the Lord qualifies."[126] Heavenly Father believes in you and trusts in your potential. Seek the Holy Ghost's guidance as you seek to know how to best prepare for your mission.

Physical Preparation Before Your Mission

Different missions have different challenges and circumstances, but regardless of where you serve, you'll need to get used to a specific sleep schedule and working long days. To prepare for this pretty intense schedule, be disciplined before your mission. Set goals, work hard, and go after your dreams!

Another part of being physically prepared is being healthy and fit. Some missions include more physical challenges than others, such as extreme weather or longer biking distances, but be ready for any area by exercising and caring for your body. Strive to eat healthy and live a balanced lifestyle as well. You can set goals now to begin your physical preparation, such as working out 3–5 days a week or sticking to a healthy bedtime routine (most missions have a 6:30 a.m. wake-up time and a 10:30 p.m. lights out).

Physical Well-Being During Your Mission:

It's important to continue caring for your health once you begin your mission. I want to emphasize this point with you because I think some hardworking sisters out there may feel it's "selfish" to take care of yourself and your health as a missionary. I'm here to tell you that it's not selfish at all! Your health is paramount! In fact, the better you take care of yourself, the stronger and more effective you'll be. Even King Benjamin in the Book of Mormon admonished his people, "See that all these things are done in wisdom and order; for it is not requisite that a man should run faster than he has strength" (Mosiah 4:27). As King Benjamin taught, we should strive to work hard while taking time to rest and take care of our bodies.

Here are a few tips regarding your physical health on your mission. First, take advantage of whatever exercise routine your mission allows. Exercising brings *so* many benefits: It can reduce stress, improve your

---

126. Thomas S. Monson, "Duty Calls," *Ensign,* May 1996, 44.

physical health, and lift your mood.[127] Sometimes though, it's tricky to work out as a missionary, depending on where you serve and things like gym access, so come to your mission prepared with workout ideas. You could:

- Bring permitted exercise equipment such as jump ropes, small weights, or a yoga mat
- Email yourself or print out specific workouts
- Choose activities that are enjoyable and will keep you motivated

If you struggle with waking up early and exercising, you could find ways to make it more fun. For example, you could play your favorite mission-approved song in the morning or give yourself a small reward if you do your workouts for a whole week. You could ask for your companion's help in keeping yourself accountable.

Or, if you're like me, you may love sports, and it may be hard not to do all the things you enjoy. It always made me extra happy when my companions were willing to run, but some were uncomfortable doing that. Get creative and do your best to get the most out of your exercise time while still working in unity with your companion.

Second, strive to eat healthy. I'd be a hypocrite if I didn't admit that I struggle with this. I even got called out as a missionary for eating too much junk food, including my favorite Nutella-flavored cereal! (I wasn't in a lot of trouble, but to improve, I had to make a healthy eating plan.) So I can say from experience that you will feel better and more readily feel the Spirit when you treat your body right. As Sister Susan W. Tanner said, "The restored gospel teaches that there is an intimate link between body, mind, and spirit. . . . When we follow the Lord's law of health for our bodies, we are also promised wisdom to our spirits and knowledge to our minds (see Doctrine and Covenants 89:19–21)."[128]

---

127. "Benefits of Exercise," NHS, Aug. 4, 2021, https://www.nhs.uk/live-well/exercise/exercise-health-benefits/.

128. Susan W. Tanner, "The Sanctity of the Body," *Ensign*, Nov. 2005, 15.

Another important point to mention is member meals (when brothers and sisters invite missionaries into their homes and prepare food for them). I loved member meals! It's been over seven years since I served, and I still can recall some of their mouthwatering dishes. However, eating member meals can be challenging for missionaries who are picky eaters or who have food allergies. Always be gracious and kind toward the brothers and sisters and the food they prepare, and be considerate of your health. Communicate any medical diets or allergies you have with the members before eating appointments so that they can be prepared.

One last, super significant suggestion is to sleep! Follow your mission's rules regarding curfew to get good rest. If you have trouble sleeping, talk to a leader for help. Remember, your health matters! Strive to care for your physical health, and you will be a stronger and more capable missionary.

There are helpful tips for your physical health in *Adjusting to Missionary Life*, a booklet you receive on your mission that helps you reduce stress. (You can also find it online on ChurchofJesusChrist.org.)[129] Many of my suggestions come from this booklet. There you will find suggestions on how to eat healthy, get good sleep, and stay motivated with exercise.

Mental and Emotional Preparation

Being a missionary is fulfilling and exciting, and it comes with many blessings, but it's also very tough! It stretches you mentally and emotionally. Richard M. Romney, in his article "Parents, Help Them to Prepare," quoted President Gordon B. Hinckley, who said, "Missionary work is not a rite of passage in the Church. It is a call extended by the President of the Church to those who are worthy and able to accomplish it. . . . There must be health and strength, both physical and mental, for the work is demanding."[130]

Your mission will be challenging, but you don't have to be daunted. Start your mental and emotional preparation now! Below is a list of suggestions on this. Check out the Study Session for more helpful

---

129. *Adjusting to Missionary Life* (2013), ChurchofJesusChrist.org.
130. Romney, "Parents, Help Them to Prepare," 40.

ideas, and let the Spirit direct you on how to best prepare and take care of your mental health, both now and during your YOMO service.

1. First, acknowledge your emotions. Pay attention to how you react to being sad, happy, bored, disappointed, and mad. Acknowledge and validate your feelings and learn how to navigate negative emotions in a healthy way. Know that this takes time!

2. Second, strive to deal with stress in healthy ways. Learn different strategies to reduce it, such as taking breaks, going on walks, listening to positive music, and doing a fun activity. Make a mental list of strategies you can do anywhere, at any time, along with hobbies you can do in your free time to squash stress and add some fun to your life!

3. Third, strive to develop a healthy mindset about your performance, growth, and failure as a daughter, student, worker, and _____ [fill in the blank with any other current life roles you may have]. Disclaimer: This was a hard one for me! As a teenager, I felt like I had to be perfect in every category of my life, from daughter to student to athlete. (And I felt so stressed out that I let one category and skill completely slide—befriending and dating boys. If you read Chapter 8, you saw how well that game plan worked out for me.) Please don't fall prey to perfectionism. Learn from your mistakes, and don't think your worth is tied to how well you do things. Your worth is *inherent* and defies physical description.

4. Fourth, remember that you don't have to be perfectly prepared to serve!

Mental and Emotional Well-Being During the Mission

Mental health disorders are common, and one in four people around the globe are affected by them,[131] so it's common for

---

131. "About Mental Illness - Clubhouse International," Clubhouse International, 2023, accessed July 25, 2024, https://clubhouse-intl.org/our-impact/about-mental-illness/.

missionaries to struggle with mental health issues too. Please know that you're not alone if you experience feelings of anxiety or depression. There is help for you. Reach out to your mission president if you're struggling with mental health. He can offer support and connect you to additional resources.

Here are a few tips for reducing stress and managing mental health as a missionary. (Note that this advice comes from my personal experience as a missionary and does not include professional advice. Seek professional help as needed.)

- When you're feeling tired or overwhelmed, take a break. It's not a sin to need breaks! It makes you human. Even the *Adjusting to Missionary Life* booklet points out that Jesus told his disciples to rest, citing Mark 6:31: "And [Jesus] said unto [His disciples], Come ye yourselves apart into a desert place, and rest a while: for there were many coming and going, and they had no leisure so much as to eat."[132] Some ideas on how to do this include taking a walk in a park, sitting down and having a quiet moment, and—dare I say it again—eating an ice cream cone after a long day of finding! Remember that resting is okay and that taking a break when needed will help you be happier and healthier, resulting in you being a more effective missionary in the long run.

- Write in your journal. You can better process your emotions through writing. As the *Adjusting to Missionary Life* booklet explains, when you write, "it helps you to at least feel understood by yourself."[133] Also, I invite you to remember that there is one person who does perfectly understand what you are feeling: the Savior. You can turn to Him in prayer for comfort and strength.

- Develop trust with companions! Seek each other's well-being and work to develop a healthy relationship. This will reduce your stress. A trusted companion can make even the hard times fun. (For more companionship tips, see chapter 14).

---

132. *Adjusting to Missionary Life* (2023), 19–20.
133. *Adjusting to Missionary Life* (2023), 34.

- You can make a music playlist with uplifting (and mission-approved) songs that can be a source of strength and comfort when you're feeling down.

- Personally, what helped me the most was getting outside of my own head, ignoring my fearful thoughts, and focusing on interacting and serving the people I was with. Was I perfect at this? No. However, listening to another person share their burdens helped me worry less about my problems, and simply spending time with others lifted my spirits.

SOCIAL PREPARATION

Oh my gosh, I have to be honest with you: I was woefully, tragically unprepared socially for my mission! I didn't know what to anticipate regarding social expectations, so I want to tell you that, as a missionary, you work with a huge variety of people, in both small and large settings. Missionary work is all about service, and it can be fun too! Here are some suggestions to help you be socially prepared for your mission:

- Call people—don't just text. Learn how to carry a conversation over the phone, not just through social media apps.

- Spend time with friends and family in person, screens down. Unless circumstances don't allow it, as a missionary, you will often interact with people face to face! While you can and should use technology to your advantage in any positive endeavor you pursue, learn how to connect with people by listening to them and putting your phone down.

- If possible, interact with people who are not your age. Personally, I have always been a little intimidated by "adults" (and still feel this way in my upper 20s), but on a mission, you will meet and possibly teach individuals of all ages, from children and teenagers to adults and the elderly. Communicate to different age groups now!

- Make new friends and branch out to meet new people. As a missionary, you'll often talk with people you haven't met before.

- Go out and serve with the missionaries. You can learn more about what to expect on a mission and can help teach a friend of the Church about the gospel.

- Serve! Take the time now to participate in service projects, help others when you see a need, and perform daily acts of kindness for strangers, friends, and family. Follow the promptings of the Spirit and reach out to those who need help or a friend.

- If you read my chapter on "Serving Before Flirting," then you already know I was woefully unprepared to serve with the opposite sex. I suggest going on dates or socializing with young men now so you are more prepared to interact with them professionally on the mission. Trust me, things will go smoother for you!

- Finally, remember that you don't have to meet these social opportunities and challenges on your own. As President Monson said, "Now, some of you may be shy by nature or consider yourselves inadequate to respond affirmatively to the call to serve. Remember that this is the Lord's work, and when we are on the Lord's errand, we are entitled to the Lord's help."[134] Have faith and trust in the Lord's divine help and strength! You can do this. You are no less meant to serve than someone else. Whether you are shy or outgoing, use your strengths, gain new ones, and turn your weaknesses over to the Lord as you serve Him.

Social Well-Being During the Mission

As a missionary, you can utilize your social skills and develop new ones! However, the social demands of a mission can be taxing at times, so here are some tips for anyone who may struggle socially as a missionary:

---

134. Thomas S. Monson, "Duty Calls," *Ensign,* May 1996, 44.

- My number one tip is to find something to enjoy about the social demands of a mission that are most challenging to you. For example, I struggled a lot with finding, which meant I needed to identify something to like about it. Eventually, I connected my love of stories with meeting new people. So when we went finding, I focused on getting to know people instead of zeroing in on my inadequacies and fear of rejection. It made it more fun!

- Second, utilize personal study! It's a time when you can reflect, ponder, and recharge your social battery. You can spend that hour strengthening your relationship with Heavenly Father and the Savior as you pray, study, seek the Spirit, and prepare to teach lessons.

- Third, take a break. If you're feeling socially exhausted, take a brief walk outside or sit down somewhere quiet and reflect. If there's no time for a break, pray in your heart for added strength to meet your responsibilities. The Lord strengthened me when I felt socially drained, and He will do the same for you.

- Fourth, communicate your needs to your companion. She can take breaks with you and respect when you need some quiet moments. It's important, though, to take time to have conversations with her and get to know her. You can be friends and support one another and, if you're like me, you can learn social skills from her!

- Fifth, if you start missing alone time and personal interests back home like I did, know that it's normal. The good news is that your service will be worth it, and your hobbies will be waiting for you when you return.

- Lastly, you can read the section "Resources for Managing Social Demands" in the *Adjusting to Missionary Life* booklet.[135] There are many helpful tips on how to communicate

---

135. *Adjusting to Missionary Life* (2023), 35–40.

with others, create needed space while obeying mission rules, and love the people you serve.

Spiritual Preparation

The intent of this section is not to give you an overwhelming to-do list but to review a few basic gospel principles that are helpful tools for life and the mission. For example, praying, studying the scriptures, and following the Spirit are essential principles taught to children that continue to guide our lives as adults. As you read the following advice, remember that gospel learning is a lifelong process. I encourage you to ponder the progress you've made, how doing these "simple" strategies has increased your faith, and what you want to get out of your gospel study in the future.

Scripture Study and Prayer

One of the greatest blessings of the mission is the time you get to spend studying and pondering God's word. Strive to create a daily habit of pondering and reading the scriptures before your mission. Nourish your testimony and seek the Spirit as you study. As the story of the sons of Mosiah in the Book of Mormon teaches us, such spiritual preparation results in spiritual power in the mission field. The sons of Mosiah had done the spiritual work to become inspired teachers to the Lamanites. Alma 17:2–3 reads:

> Now these sons of Mosiah were with Alma at the time the angel first appeared unto him; therefore Alma did rejoice exceedingly to see his brethren; and what added more to his joy, they were still his brethren in the Lord; yea, and they had waxed strong in the knowledge of the truth; for they were men of a sound understanding and they had searched the scriptures diligently, that they might know the word of God.
>
> But this is not all; they had given themselves to much prayer, and fasting; therefore they had the spirit of prophecy, and the spirit of revelation, and when they taught, they taught with power and authority of God.

Because the sons of Mosiah had diligently and prayerfully studied God's word, they were spiritually prepared missionaries. They were blessed to teach "with the power and authority of God." We can all follow the pattern set by the sons of Mosiah. Start your spiritual feasting now. It's never too late to start!

However, don't just develop a daily habit of scripture study and prayer to be prepared to serve a mission. Increase your knowledge of the gospel because you want to know the truth for yourself. Discover what "the joy of Christ" means to you (Alma 31:38). As President Uchtdorf taught, your witness of the truth "will enlighten your mind," "bring healing . . . and joy to your days," and will bless you throughout eternity.[136] I know that my knowledge of the gospel has given me hope and happiness.

Seek the Spirit

As you study God's word and build your testimony, remember to seek the guidance and companionship of the Holy Ghost. Start learning now how the Holy Ghost speaks to you. Engage in activities that invite the Spirit into your life, such as worshiping in the temple, sincerely serving others, and watching uplifting media. As President Nelson counseled us, "I plead with you to increase your spiritual capacity to receive revelation. . . . Choose to do the spiritual work required to enjoy the gift of the Holy Ghost and hear the voice of the Spirit more frequently and more clearly."[137]

Strive to have the Spirit with you. Write down the promptings you receive as you study God's word, remembering that "by the power of the Holy Ghost ye may know the truth of all things" (Moroni 10:5). Courageously act on the promptings you receive. Nothing will be more important on your mission than following the Spirit.

Receive and Review Your Patriarchal Blessing

When you're ready, you can also pray about and ask to receive your patriarchal blessing. Or, if you already have it, you can continue to prayerfully study it. Many blessings come from doing so. For

---

136. Dieter F. Uchtdorf, "Receiving a Testimony of Light and Truth," *Ensign* or *Liahona*, Nov. 2014, 23.

137. Russell M. Nelson, "Revelation for the Church, Revelation for Our Lives," *Ensign* or *Liahona*, May 2018, 96.

example, Elder Randall K. Bennett testified that his patriarchal blessing enabled him to see his divine identity, which caused him to want to do more of what Heavenly Father asks of him.[138] Personally, my patriarchal blessing has given me fresh insight about my problems. It reminds me to have an eternal perspective and to talk to and trust God more.

Attend the Temple

Worshiping in the temple can also help you have an eternal perspective and "think celestial," as President Nelson has invited us to do.[139] He said, "[The temple] is His House. It is filled with His power. . . . I promise that increased time in the temple will bless your life in ways nothing else can."[140] Whenever I attend the temple, I feel peace and a reminder of Heavenly Father and the Savior's love for us. I invite you to follow President Nelson's counsel and worship in the temple and access its power and blessings more often. If you have not received your temple endowment, prayerfully consider when to receive it. Some sisters have found it helpful to receive their endowment a couple of months before their missions so that they can attend the temple a few times before they go. Follow the Spirit's promptings and do whatever is best for you and your circumstances.

Learn About the Priesthood

A final suggestion for preparing spiritually is to learn more about the priesthood. Understanding the priesthood better will empower you as a missionary and a disciple of Christ, and the prophet himself has counseled us to learn more about it. President Nelson encouraged sisters to "study prayerfully *all* the truths you can find about priesthood power" and cited Doctrine and Covenants 84 and 107 as great starting points.[141] I encourage you to follow the prophet's invitation. President Nelson added, "How I yearn for you to understand that the

---

138. Randall K. Bennett, "Your Patriarchal Blessing—Inspired Direction from Heavenly Father," *Liahona*, May 2023, 42–43.
139. Russell M. Nelson, "Think Celestial!," *Liahona*, Nov. 2023, 117–19.
140. Russell M. Nelson, "Focus on the Temple," *Liahona*, Nov. 2022, 121.
141. Russell M. Nelson, "Spiritual Treasures," *Ensign* or *Liahona*, Nov. 2019, 79.

restoration of the priesthood is just as relevant to you as a woman as it is to any man." I love that!

As you begin your study of the priesthood and missionary preparation, I'd like to give you a basic outline of a few essential concepts. First, the priesthood is the "power and authority of God," and "in mortality," the priesthood is "the power and authority that God gives to man to act in all things necessary for the salvation of God's children."[142] Second, men are not the priesthood. Rather, they are ordained to priesthood offices and authorized to administer ordinances. This doesn't make men superior to anyone else in the Church, but it actually means that they are called to follow the Savior's example and to humbly serve others (Matthew 20:26). Third, while women are not ordained to offices of the priesthood, they can (and should) be seeking its power in their daily lives. A woman can access priesthood authority and power through both callings and covenants. President Nelson explained that you receive priesthood authority when you are set apart to serve in a calling and that if you have been endowed in the temple, you have access to priesthood power. He said, "Those who are endowed in the house of the Lord receive a gift of God's priesthood power by virtue of their covenant, along with a gift of knowledge to know how to draw upon that power."[143]

Reflect upon and follow President Nelson's invitation to utilize that power more often. That priesthood power is available to us as we live in harmony with the gospel, are worthy, and are faithful to our covenants. Fourth, for both a man and a woman, a fulness of priesthood blessings is obtained only through the culminating ordinance of the temple sealing. To sum it up, as a missionary, you are called to serve with priesthood authority, and through the temple endowment, you can access priesthood power.

Remember, you are a daughter of a King! The Spirit will testify of this sacred and beautiful truth to you as you pray and study His word through the scriptures, modern-day prophets, and your patriarchal blessing. Start spiritually preparing for your life's mission now by repenting daily, keeping your covenants, worshipping in the temple,

---

142. Topics and Questions, "Priesthood," Gospel Library.
143. Russell M. Nelson, "Spiritual Treasures," 77.

strengthening your faith in the gospel of Christ, and accessing God's power in your life.

Spiritual Well-Being During the Mission

On your mission, you will have scheduled time for studying God's word, both on your own and with your companion. Appreciate and utilize this time you have to study the gospel of Christ. As Elder Bednar counseled missionaries in the Provo MTC, "Treasure up the words of eternal life." He explained, "Treasuring up the words of eternal life is more than merely studying or memorizing, just as 'feasting upon the word[s] of Christ' (2 Nephi 31:20; see also 2 Nephi 32:3) is more than simply sampling or snacking. Treasuring up suggests to me focusing and working, exploring and absorbing, pondering and praying, applying and learning, valuing and appreciating, and enjoying and relishing."[144]

I must confess that sometimes it's easy to turn my scripture study into a checklist instead of a spiritual feast. However, as Elder Bednar admonished, really seek to understand God's word. Ask questions. Highlight scriptures that speak to you. Write down spiritual impressions you receive. You can also use a myriad of resources to enhance your study, such as institute manuals, older conference talks, *Jesus the Christ* by Elder James E. Talmage, and the Bible Dictionary.

In addition to the scriptures and conference talks, you can diligently study *Preach My Gospel*, your guide to the work. I wish I had taken better advantage of *Preach My Gospel*'s resources and tools. You can also prayerfully find and ponder scriptures that will help the people you teach. As a missionary, I invite you to keep reading and pondering your patriarchal blessing as well. It can be helpful to remember that God has a purpose for your life outside the mission. This reminder of the bigger picture can give you hope and inspire you.

In my finisher's letter, I wrote, "I know that the Book of Mormon is true. Study the Book of Mormon and scriptures daily—it *will* save you. It saved me on the mission! When I not only read but studied the

---

144. David A. Bednar, "Becoming a *Preach My Gospel* Missionary," *New Era*, Oct. 2013, 2.

scriptures with the Spirit, I received amazing inspiration and knowledge and had a better day." God's word will empower you.

Additionally, seek to follow the Spirit. This is the most crucial point of all. God has promised you the Holy Ghost as your constant companion (see Moroni 4:2–3; Moroni 5). Through the Spirit, you can receive communication from our Heavenly Father.[145] As Sister Cristina B. Franco said, "Heavenly Father . . . knows who you are and what you need. He hears and answers your prayers. No matter how lonely you feel, He's always there. You are never alone. You can always turn to Him."[146]

Heavenly Father knows you personally. He knows your quirks, strengths, weaknesses, trials, and triumphs. Because of this, His Spirit is the most important resource and guide because no one knows you better, wants you to succeed more, and knows how to best help you succeed than your Heavenly Father. YOMO by seeking the Spirit and accepting the Lord's help.

In my finisher's letter, I wrote, "I must be honest—at times, I've doubted and feared and fought against the Spirit, which has only brought me more problems and sins. But listening to the Spirit has saved me and enabled me to serve others better and just be more successful. The thing is, sometimes in the moment it's harder to follow the promptings of the Spirit, but later it's easier if you do. The Spirit is always right." Honestly, sisters, it's still hard for me to follow the Holy Ghost sometimes. I'm stubborn and sometimes think my ideas are better. But I know that if we exercise faith and follow the promptings we receive, the Spirit will steer us in the right direction. We will always end up on a path to something more beautiful and majestic than we can imagine.

A Note on Preparation

My goal with this chapter is to provide practical advice on how to be prepared for a mission and hopefully help you be more prepared than I was! The First Presidency has said that "missionaries are

---

145. See Dallin H. Oaks, "Two Lines of Communication," *Ensign* or *Liahona*, Nov. 2010, 83–86.
146. Cristina B. Franco, "Heavenly Father Knows You," *Friend*, June 2018.

most likely to experience success when they are worthy and physically, mentally, and emotionally prepared for missionary service."[147] That said, I think Church leaders would agree that "prepared" doesn't mean perfect. It means striving and learning all you can and implementing what you learn, one principle at a time. Please don't feel like you must tackle everything at once or ace everything right now! Keep setting goals, but don't impose unrealistic expectations or unnecessary deadlines on yourself. You don't have just before or after your mission to improve—you have your entire life. You got this, future YOMO sisters!

ADDITIONAL TIPS DURING YOUR MISSION

TIP #1: KEEP A JOURNAL (OR TWO)

On your mission, you'll receive spiritual promptings to help lead others (and yourself) closer to Christ. You'll also have certain experiences that are meant to teach you personally and are messages from God for your life. Treasure these divine messages! Write down these spiritual insights. President Spencer W. Kimball counseled, "What could you do better for your children and your children's children than to record the story of your life, your triumphs over adversity, your recovery after a fall, your progress when all seemed black, your rejoicing when you had finally achieved? . . . Maybe the angels may quote from it for eternity."[148]

Your mission experiences are definitely something that your future family would want to read about! Recording your challenges, lessons, and achievements will be invaluable to you and your family. I have looked back on my missionary journal and received insight and counsel from my younger self.

Additionally, I recommend creating your own system for recording experiences. Don't feel like you have to do it my way, but to get you thinking, I had one journal called my "vent" journal where I could freely express my honest feelings about everything. It was therapeutic

---

147. Romney, "Parents, Help Them to Prepare," 40.
148. Dean Jessee, "The Power of Personal Journals Is Enduring," *Church News*, Jan. 21, 2015.

for me. I had another journal called my "Tender Mercies Journal" in which I wrote down a couple of positive experiences or a divine blessing from that day. My "vent" journal was helpful in the moment, but post-mission, what I really adore is my beautiful, teal "Tender Mercies Journal" that contains all the heart, beauty, and blessings of my mission. One day, when you come home, you will be delighted to read about your past spiritual experiences and excited to look back on the most cherished memories from your mission. YOMO by keeping a journal of those memories and being an inspiration to your future self and your future family, as President Kimball mentioned.

#2: *Foreign Language Help (If Called to Speak a Different Language)*

Learning a foreign language is *not* easy, but the Lord will bless you as you give your best efforts. The gift of tongues is real, but it doesn't usually work like magic. You will need to practice the language and put in the work. However, the Holy Ghost will magnify your sincere efforts to learn the language. Here are a few more language-learning tips:

- Make sure to practice all aspects of the language. As a missionary, I made the mistake of not working on my pronunciation and accent because it was uncomfortable. As a result, I had, and still have, a strong American accent when I speak German. Focus on what you feel inspired to do or what the mission president directs you to do, but most likely, it will be important to work on all components of the language, including learning vocabulary, pronunciation, grammar, and cultural cues. Don't be like me and fail to grow in one aspect of the language! Strive to grow in all language areas.

- Beyond following the Spirit and mission rules, here are some additional ideas to sharpen your language skills: 1. Speak as often as possible in the foreign language (we had German-speaking-only rules in our mission for certain meetings, times, and places). 2. Read the scriptures in the foreign language (unless directed to read them in your native tongue). 3. Master gospel-related words that you use in lessons, and take time to learn other vocabulary (such as food, daily life, culture, etc.) to better connect with people and begin natural conversations with them. As Elder Holland said, "Don't be satisfied with what we call a missionary vocabulary only. Stretch yourself in the language, and you will gain greater access to the hearts of the people."[149]

- Be patient with yourself! Learning a foreign language can be stressful, and especially in your first few months, it may feel overwhelming. Know that it takes most missionaries some time to adjust to the language, so you are normal if you freak out at first. After a few months, it slowly starts to click, and then you're able to improve at a more rapid pace, so don't give up! As *Preach My Gospel* says, "Part of seeking the gift of tongues is to labor and do all you can to learn the language. Be patient as you prayerfully study and practice the language. Trust that the Spirit will help you as you make a diligent effort. Have faith that you can have the gift of tongues to help you and those you teach."[150] Chapter 7 of *Preach My Gospel* provides many useful tips on language learning and the gift of tongues.

- Make it fun! This is an important point. Although learning a new language is difficult, embrace the challenge. It can be enjoyable and satisfying to progress in a language. For example, I loved looking up new vocabulary words and using them in conversations. (It may sound silly, but one of my most gratifying moments on the mission was when I looked up how to say "menstrual cycle" in German, and then the phrase came in handy a few days later.) You can make language learning enjoyable by creating practice games, setting goals, and celebrating small victories with your companion. It becomes especially fun and meaningful when you incorporate culture. Don't just learn the language, but learn about the people and their history. People will be touched that you're taking the

---

149. *Preach My Gospel*, 140.
150. *Preach My Gospel*, 143.

time to learn about their culture and their language. As *Preach My Gospel* says, "One of the greatest things you can do to gain people's trust and love is to respect and embrace their culture in appropriate ways."[151] Your curiosity, dedication, and love can open doors!

YOMO Activity: Preparing to Serve

There was a lot of information in this chapter! Don't feel overwhelmed—I'm sure you're more prepared than you realize. I invite you to choose one goal from one of the preparation sections that stood out to you and make a plan to work on it. Only pick one!

Study Session: Preparing to Serve

- Ezra Taft Benson, "Preparing Yourselves for Missionary Service," *Ensign*, May 1985, 36–37.

- Dieter F. Uchtdorf, "Receiving a Testimony of Light and Truth," *Ensign* or *Liahona*, Nov. 2014, 20–23.

- Randall K. Bennett, "Your Patriarchal Blessing—Inspired Direction from Heavenly Father," *Liahona*, May 2023, 42–43.

- Robert K. Wagstaff, "Preparing Emotionally for Missionary Service," *Ensign*, March 2011, 22–26.

- Caleb N. Porter, "Dear Future Missionaries," *New Era*, Oct. 2012.

- Wendy Ulrich, "The Hardest Part of Being a Missionary," *New Era*, June 2016.

- Start studying *Preach My Gospel* and learning more about missionary work from the prophet and apostles.

- Learn more about the priesthood by reading Barbara Morgan Gardner, *The Priesthood Power of Women: In the Temple, Church, and Family* (Salt Lake City, UT: Deseret Book, 2019),

---

151. *Preach My Gospel*, 143.

or by listening to Dr. Barbara Gardner on the *Follow Him* podcast, "Episode 31 Part 1–2: Doctrine & Covenants 84."

- Mosiah 4:27; Alma 17:2–3, 9–12

17

How to YOMO After Your Mission

It may seem like your life is more like *The RM* than *The Notebook*, but I promise it'll all work out.

"Jesus Christ has overcome the world. And because of Him, because of His infinite Atonement, we all have great cause to trust, knowing that ultimately all will be well." —Bonnie H. Cordon[152]

Post-Mission Life

In late August of 2017, I flew home from Berlin to Indiana, rocking an awkwardly long pixie cut, excited to see family again, and eager to start my new life back home. During the first two weeks of returning to Indiana, there were many happy moments as I spent time with my family, sharing mission stories and seeing my dad beam with pride

---

152. Bonnie H. Cordon, "Trust in the Lord and Lean Not," *Ensign* or *Liahona*, May 2017, 9.

over my service. Then I flew to Utah and started my fourth semester at Brigham Young University, and the rest of my life began.

The rest of my life was great, but there were some rocky parts too. Here were some moments of transition for me:

- **Preaching 24/7 to studying 24/7.** I'd always loved being a student, but it was weird to go from being with people all the time to spending many hours studying solo. (I was a little bit of a crazy straight-A student and probably didn't have to spend so much time studying, but it's what I chose.) So to ease the transition, I recommend still prioritizing relationships and service, even while continuing your education, career, or other endeavors.

- **Going on a run.** Literally one day after I returned home, I grabbed my tennis shoes and headphones and headed outside to go run on our country road surrounded by corn fields. It was a hot, humid August afternoon. My mom called out to me, "Are you comfortable running alone again?" I nodded and sprinted off. No trouble getting back into that hobby! While it had been worth it to give up certain activities for eighteen months, such as running alone, it was fun to start doing them again!

- **Missing mission life.** I can't say I missed everything about mission life, but I definitely missed the adventure of it all and especially the people. I messaged one of my friends from Germany frequently, and she seemed to sense that I was struggling to move on. She told me, "Live your life. Don't dwell in the past. Move forward and focus on your life back in the United States." While it's normal and okay to miss the mission, you gotta YOLO and live in the present!

- **Dating.** (You know I had to include this!) For the first few months back at BYU, dating was an adjustment because going from "don't date as a missionary" to "flirt, date, and get married" was a lot. One of my first dates back home was at BYU's Museum of Art on campus. Dozens of couples thronged the building, analyzing and enjoying paintings, sculptures, and other works of art. My date and I were walking past drawings framed in gold when he suddenly looked at me and started holding my hand! Surprised, I felt myself vacillate quickly between emotions, like a ping pong ball bouncing back and forth: first, thrilled that a boy liked me, then confused because I wasn't sure yet how much I liked him; and then guilty because a guy was holding my hand! It felt like I was breaking a rule. I chanted mentally to myself, "You aren't a missionary anymore—this is fine!" I survived the hand-holding that evening, and eventually, interacting with boys became more normal, and I was able to have a perfectly imperfect dating experience!

Sisters, even though transitioning back to "normal life" was difficult at times, I'm grateful for my mission. I know that my experience as a missionary in the Germany Berlin Mission was a complete game-changer for me. It shaped my goals and desires and strengthened my character and my faith. I have seen many blessings in my life due to my service, and I know that God is pleased with the sacrifice I gave, even though I wasn't always perfect. Take comfort in God's love for you, and know that He will bless you and help guide you through your life transitions.

YOMO Tips: Adjusting to Life After the Mission

I want to share with you a few tips to remember as you return to your life back home. First, remember that your experience will be different than mine. For example, you may focus on a career instead of school. What was difficult for me may be easier for you and vice versa. Just know that although we each have different experiences, we sisters can rally together and support one another.

Second, I want you to give yourself grace as you enter your new "normal" life. You will likely want to maintain the positive habits you developed on the mission such as daily scripture study—and I encourage you to do so—but you may find it challenging to implement those habits when you're back in the world of work, school, socializing, finances, and a billion other commitments. Please be patient with yourself as you make and set goals. You may need to adapt some habits and goals into your new busy schedule, such as studying the scriptures for ten minutes instead of an hour or two a day. Just do your best, and don't be hard on yourself!

Third, along with maintaining positive habits, cherish and remember your mission. Read your mission journals and the faith-building, sacred experiences you had. Continue to build your testimony. However, as my friend reminded me, don't dwell in the past. There can be a temptation to stay put in what's comfortable, meaning living in the memories of your mission and focusing your mind on the past instead of diving into the future ahead of you. I invite you to move forward with faith because the Lord has great things in store for you. As President Monson said, "The future is as bright as your faith."[153] Your opportunities for blessings and service don't end with the mission. If you want it, God will continue to use you to do His work. As mission leaders Marianna and Steve Richardson wrote, "Your mission was not meant to be the best eighteen months or two years of your life; instead, it was meant to be the beginning of a wonderful, Spirit-filled adult life."[154] Your future can be faith-filled and miraculous too, just like your mission.

Fourth, trust your Heavenly Father. That isn't always easy, but I know that God loves you, is pleased with your service, and will bless you. Trust in His promises. He wants you to be happy. So after returning home, pursue your dreams! Do what you love. One of my mission companions wrote in my Tschüss book, "You can do anything you want. Be anything you dream. God has a plan for you, yes, but He is very mindful of what you want as well, just like any loving father would be." Be hopeful about the future. Remember that just as "God did not send you here to fail" on the mission, He didn't send you here to fail on your earthly mission either. He will strengthen, uplift, and cheer you on.

Fifth, I want you to know that it's okay if everything doesn't go according to plan after you return home. If you have ever watched the super cheesy comedy *The RM* ("returned missionary"), you know

---

153. Thomas S. Monson, "Be of Good Cheer," *Ensign* or *Liahona*, May 2009, 92.
154. Marianna and Steve Richardson, "8 Ways to Stay Strong After Your Mission," *Liahona*, Sept. 2022.

what I'm talking about. The film's basic message is that not everything turns out the way we want them to or when we want them to. Obviously, it's easier to write about this truth than to act on it. I personally think my plans are pretty great, and it's very frustrating when they don't all line up neatly on the pages of my life book like obedient soldiers in formation. However, I know God has all wisdom, power, and knowledge (see Mosiah 4:6, 9). As Proverbs 3:5–6 reads, "Trust in the Lord with all thine heart; and lean not unto thine own understanding. In all thy ways acknowledge him, and he shall direct thy paths." It can be difficult trusting God's plan more than our own, but I know that even when things don't work out perfectly (such as a ring by spring), or some things make you feel like a fish out of water (flirting again), eventually all things will work out through God's mercy and grace. Turn your YOMO into a healthy YOLO! You only live once, so live in the present, do your best, and have joy through Christ. Your life will be great!

YOMO Activity: New Changes

Ponder a transition you've experienced in your life. Reflect on the following questions, and either write down your thoughts in a journal or discuss them with a friend or parent.

1. What is one transition that you've experienced in your life?
2. What was difficult about the transition?
3. What did you enjoy about it?
4. What helped you embrace the new changes in your life?
5. Although you will face new challenges and opportunities as a missionary, how could the lessons you learned from this transition help you as you first go on a mission and then return back home?

Study Session: Keep YOMOing, Sister!

- Bonnie H. Cordon, "Trust in the Lord and Lean Not," *Ensign* or *Liahona*, May 2017, 6–9.

- Breanne Su'a, "Finding My New Normal after My Mission," Liahona, Feb. 2021.

- Marianna and Steve Richardson, "8 Ways to Stay Strong after Your Mission," *Liahona*, Sept. 2022.

- Liahona Ficquet, "Early-Returned Missionaries: You Aren't Alone," *Ensign*, July 2019.

- Alex Hugie, "If Your Mission Ended Early, Don't Give Up," *Ensign,* July 2019.

- Alma 15:16–18; Doctrine and Covenants 88:76–80; 2 Nephi 31:16–21; Proverbs 3:5–6

18

BLESSINGS FROM SERVING

The Lord is proud of you and will bless you for your service.

"Some blessings come soon, some come late, and some don't come until heaven; but for those who embrace the gospel of Jesus Christ, they come." —Elder Jeffrey R. Holland[155]

BLESSINGS FROM SERVING A MISSION

My mission changed the course of my life. I know that sounds dramatic, but it's true. Many blessings and opportunities have come into my life because of my experiences as a missionary. In this chapter, I want to share with you some of these blessings, but I don't want to send the message that someone can only receive blessings if they serve a mission, because that's not true. There are many ways to serve the Lord. However, a mission was part of God's plan for me.

Since my mission, I have graduated from Brigham Young University with a bachelor's degree in English and German and a master's degree in sociology. I married my husband in the Payson Utah

---

155. Jeffrey R. Holland, "An High Priest of Good Things to Come," *Ensign*, November 1999, 38.

Temple, and I teach sociology classes at a local community college. I have had the opportunity to travel, meet new people, and explore my hobbies and interests. I have been blessed with great friendships and helpful mentors. I mention all these blessings and opportunities not to brag—since I could also list all the trials and troubles in between, from dating fails to stressful semesters to continued challenges—but I mention them to show you that they all have been influenced by or are a direct result of my missionary service.

Many of the blessings I mentioned above have come about due to the personal growth I experienced on my mission. Here are some examples of the growth I experienced and the blessings that came from it. (You could make your own list after your mission!)

- **Social growth.** Speaking and teaching with people helped me become more confident and taught me social skills. This has helped me connect with more people, and yes, it helped me flirt with boys and have a fun YSA experience!

- **Spiritual growth.** I experienced tender mercies on my mission and learned more about our Savior and His gospel. My testimony was strengthened. My faith has helped me make decisions, face challenges, and feel joy.

- **Life skills.** I've heard other missionaries say it too: The mission is an intense training program—a mini precursor of what life is like. You get a crash course on how to best live the rest of your life! You learn what really matters and how living the gospel of Christ brings the greatest happiness.

- **Cultural skills.** Interacting with people from different countries and of different religions helped me be more aware of other cultures and learn how to work with people from different backgrounds than my own. This is a valuable skill for life and for the workplace!

- **Rejection.** On your mission, you'll get rejected. Not everyone will want to hear the gospel message. However, one blessing from this is that you learn not to let rejection stop you! Not letting rejection stop me has empowered me to send that email, make that phone call, go on that date, and try that new opportunity. I have had more fun and more life experiences because of this principle.

- **Connections.** One of the most special blessings of serving a mission is the people you meet and the relationships you build. I'm grateful for the ward members in Germany, for their examples of faith and love. I'm grateful for our friends of the Church who I learned from just as much as I taught them. I'm grateful for the people we met on the street who touched my life for just a brief moment with their wise words and kindness. All these friendships and connections showed me how much more vibrant and colorful life can be as we open ourselves up to people and love them.

- Your list of blessings will likely be similar but also uniquely catered to you!

While I've received many blessings because of my mission, it's also important to note that we don't all receive blessings in the same way or on the same timeline we expect. After your mission, if you feel like you are facing more trials than triumphs, know that you aren't doing anything wrong. Life is simply full of challenges. But I know that God loves each of us, and in His way and timing, He will bless you for your service. Hebrews 6:10 reads, "For God is not unrighteous to forget your work and labour of love, which ye have shewed toward his name, in that ye have ministered to the saints, and do minister."

I love that glorious promise! Nothing will bring you more blessings than serving the Lord, and there are many ways to do so. I don't regret serving a mission; it has changed my life and has given me more confidence and happiness than any other experience. I hope we can trust the Lord and embark on our unique journeys with faith and love.

YOMO Activity: Reflect On Missions

After nearly finishing this book, what is something that you have learned about missions? Has anything surprised you? What do you think you'll find most challenging, and what do you think you'll find most rewarding? Share your insights and questions with a parent or trusted adult.

Study Session: Blessings That Come from Serving a Mission

- M. Russell Ballard, "Missionary Service Blessed My Life Forever," *Liahona*, May 2022, 8–10.
- James M. Dunn, "The Blessings of Missionary Service," *Ensign*, Nov. 1983, 34–36.
- David F. Evans, "The Blessings of Missionary Service," *Liahona* (Asia Area Leader Message), Feb. 2019.
- Mindy Selu, "3 Unexpected Blessings of Serving a Mission," *YA Weekly*, May 2022.
- Hebrews 6:10; Isaiah 52:7; Alma 19:14; Alma 26; Doctrine and Covenants 6:9; 18:15; 118:3

Final Letter

Dear readers,

I hope that reading this little book of mine gave you hope and excitement for your life and your possible future missions. Whether you decide to serve a mission or not, please know that Heavenly Father loves you and has great plans for your future, glorious beyond your imagination. He wants to help you reach your divine potential as His daughter. Pray to Heavenly Father and ask for a witness of His love and eternal plan for you.

If you do decide to serve a mission, I hope my experiences help you feel a little more confident (although it's normal to still be nervous!) to go out and "preach the gospel to every creature" (Mark 16:15), remembering that you don't have to be perfect to be a good missionary. God expects us to strive to give our best effort, and as we turn to the Lord, the Savior can magnify our efforts. Remember that the Savior is always there for you, waiting for you to turn to Him and ask for His divine grace and help. "I will not leave you comfortless: I will come to you," Jesus promises (John 14:18). Readily accept the Savior's help and seek guidance from the Holy Ghost. The Spirit will be your indispensable guide, comforter, and teacher as you embark on this great work of salvation (see John 14:16).[156]

Also, don't forget to YOMO! Embrace the principles of "you only mission once" so that you can serve to the fullest! This is a special and sacred time in your life when you get to devote all your energy to serving the Lord and sharing His gospel. At times, it may seem like all that exists is your life and schedule as a missionary, but before you know it, the time will be gone and a new stage of life will hit you like an oncoming train. So enjoy the mission! I challenge you to fully commit to your role as a missionary. It took me way too long to do so. Missionary work is kind of like skiing; you have to commit to the thrill and the possibility of falling down to fully enjoy the feeling of flying and soaring down the mountain.

Strive to have fun on your mission; build connections with your companions, ward members, and the people you teach; and live with hope, purpose, and faith. Friends and family on both sides of the veil will cheer you on. Only Satan wants you to fail, but he has already lost. As Elder Holland said, "There is absolutely no question as to who wins because victory has already been posted on the scoreboard. The only really strange thing in all of this is that we are still down here on the field trying to decide which team's jersey we want to wear!"[157] Righteousness will prevail, and God will help us succeed on our earthly missions (1 Nephi 3:7; Doctrine and Covenants 84:88).

Live your destiny. Your story doesn't have to look like anyone else's. We have all been given divine traits and gifts that we can use to serve others and fulfill our earthly missions.[158] Remember that you are good enough to serve a mission. You are enough for the Lord, and with the Savior's help, you can become the disciple you are meant to be. Build your testimony of Christ and His gospel, and discover your

---

156. Topics and Questions, "Holy Ghost," Gospel Library. See also Gospel Topics, "Holy Ghost," Gospel Library.

157. "Jeffrey R. Holland | Quotes | Quotable Quote," Goodreads, accessed May 29, 2023. https://www.goodreads.com/quotes/303294-the-future-of-this-world-has-long-been-declared-the.

158. Guide to the Scriptures, "Gifts of the Spirit," Gospel Library.

true worth as a daughter of God. You'll do great as a future missionary. Just don't forget to YOMO!

>Wishing you the best YOMO and YOLO life ever,
>Hannah

PS: Lessons I Learned from My Mission to Apply to My Post-Mission Life

(I invite you to make your own list after your mission! Include principles that will help you continue to YOMO and live life to its fullest.)

1. Live your life with these five words: passion, purpose, faith, hope, and charity (see Moroni 7:40–48).
2. Don't take life or yourself too seriously.
3. Have fun with friends, build connections with people, and learn from others.
4. Keep progressing, but don't demand perfection (see Mosiah 4:27).
5. Be obedient and keep the commandments and your covenants; you will be protected from spiritual danger.
6. Communication is *key* in relationships.
7. Forgive others, and remember to forgive yourself too.
8. Prayer and scripture power are real.
9. Believe in angels.
10. Heavenly Father and Jesus Christ are our sources of strength.

PPS: My Testimony of Christ and His Gospel

Sisters, I'd like to share my testimony that I know that Jesus is the Christ. He died for us, overcame death, and atoned for our sins. The Savior loves us and can truly be with us during our times of trial and temptation. Heavenly Father loves us too, and we are all equal in His sight—His daughters with an unimaginably wonderful future and divine destiny. I know that the Book of Mormon is the word of God and that the Spirit can speak to us as we read and study it.

It's sometimes hard for me to follow the Holy Ghost's promptings, but I know that only positive endings come from listening to the Spirit and acting on such inspiration. I know that our families are important to God and that we can be with our families for eternity through the Savior's Atonement and God's plan. I don't have all the answers to how everything will work out or why we have to go through certain trials, but I know that God loves us. I know that Heavenly Father loves you, His courageous, valiant, and beautiful daughters. I know that because of Christ and His sacrifice and victory, we can have hope in this world. We can have peace and joy through Christ.

Appendix A
History of the Germany Berlin Mission and the Freiberg Temple

A Brief History of Missionary Work in Germany

All information listed here from 1840–1990 can be found on the timeline on the Church's website titled "German: Chronology."[159]

- 1840: The first missionary to set foot on German soil was an English man named James Howard.

- 1843: The first branch was established in Germany, in Darmstadt, by Johann Greenig, a German convert.

- 1852: The first Book of Mormon in German was published in Hamburg. The Hamburg Branch was formed in the same year.

- 1868: Switzerland and Germany became a new mission in The Church of Jesus Christ of Latter-day Saints.

---

159. "Church History | German: Chronology," The Church of Jesus Christ of Latter-day Saints, accessed July 25, 2024, https://www.churchofjesuschrist.org/study/history/global-histories/germany/de-chronology.

- 1884: In Berlin, the first Relief Society group was created, with Pauline Kowallis as president.

- 1914–1918: During World War I (1914–1918), the work of salvation continued as local members served missions and 500 people were baptized in Germany.

- 1933–1945: Leading up to and during World War II, the Nazi Party seized Church literature, forbade Church meetings to be held during party rallies, and interrogated members. A seventeen-year-old member named Helmuth Hübener spread pamphlets against Nazi propaganda and was killed, and two other teenagers who helped him were sent to labor camps.

- 1949–1989: After World War II, Germany was divided into West and East Germany, with the Allied Nations controlling the West and Russia controlling the East.

- 1960: The European Mission was reorganized with Frankfurt at its center, and the first stake in Germany was established in Berlin just a year later.

- 1982: The first stake in the German Democratic Republic (GDR) was formed in Freiberg and led by Frank Herbert Apel.

- 1985: The Freiberg Temple was dedicated by President Thomas S. Monson, who was serving as an Apostle at the time.

- 1989: The first foreign missionaries served in the GDR for the first time in fifty years.

- 1990: East and West Germany were reunited.

- 2000: At this time, there were six separate missions in Germany.[160]

- 2010: The Hamburg and Berlin missions combined to form the Germany Berlin Mission, and Munich/Austria, Zurich,

---

160. Paul VanDenBerghe, "A Foundation of Strength in Germany," *Ensign*, Aug. 2000.

and parts of the Frankfurt mission combined to form the Alpine German-Speaking Mission.[161]

- July 1, 2024: Hamburg once again became its own mission, making Germany home to the Frankfurt, Berlin, Munich, and Hamburg missions.[162]

THE INSPIRING STORY OF THE FREIBERG GERMANY TEMPLE

The story of the Freiberg Temple is not really mine to share. It belongs to the faithful Saints who lived in the Russian-occupied German Democratic Republic (GDR) after World War II and the members in Germany today. However, I will share a brief history of the Freiberg Temple because it's a miraculous testament to God's power and the faith of the Saints in Germany. My mission would have been incomplete without this temple. During its rededication and open house, I had the opportunity to volunteer with the other sisters and feel the special spirit there. The brief history I'll share is based on the article by David F. Boone and Richard O. Cowan entitled "The Freiberg Germany Temple: A Latter-day Miracle."[163] (Every fact and quote in this summary can be attributed to Boone and Cowan. Local leaders gave all of the sister missionaries this article to read in connection with the second dedication of the Freiberg Germany Temple on September 4, 2016.)

After World War II, the saints in the GDR were cut off from the rest of the world. Undaunted, the German Saints continued to live with faith, and hundreds of people were baptized into The Church of Jesus Christ of Latter-day Saints. However, due to government restrictions, the Saints could not travel to the temple in Switzerland. When serving as an Apostle, President Thomas S. Monson visited

---

161. "Church Makes Mission Changes," *Ensign*, July 2010, 76.
162. Scott Taylor, "With 36 new missions coming in 2024, get to know the cities, states and countries a little better," *Church News*, Nov. 8, 2023.
163. David F. Boone and Richard O. Cowan, "The Freiberg Germany Temple: A Latter-day Miracle" in *Regional Studies in Latter-day Saint Church History: Europe*, ed. Donald Q. Cannon and Brent L. Top (Provo, UT: BYU Religious Studies Center, 2003), 147–67.

> **Temple Timeline**[1]
>
> **April 23, 1983**
> Groundbreaking of the Freiberg Temple
>
> **June 29, 1985**
> The Freiberg Temple was dedicated by President Hinckley
>
> **September 7, 2002**
> Rededication of the Freiberg Temple by President Hinckley
>
> **September 4, 2016**
> Second rededication of the Freiberg Temple by President Uchtdorf
>
> ---
>
> 1. Facts retrieved from "Freiberg Germany Temple," *Newsroom*, accessed July 25, 2024, ChurchofJesusChrist.org; "President Dieter F. Uchtdorf Rededicates Freiberg Germany Temple," *Newsroom*, Sept. 4, 2016, ChurchofJesusChrist.org.

these members and felt compassion for their situation, seeing they were without patriarchs, wards, stakes, or opportunities to attend the temple. He noted that despite these difficulties, "they trusted in the Lord with all their hearts."[164] Boone and Cowan wrote, "With great feeling he [Elder Monson] promised them: 'If you will remain true and faithful to the commandments of God, every blessing any member of the Church enjoys in any other country will be yours.'"[165]

In 1973, Walter Krause was ordained a patriarch under the leadership of President Burkhardt, the leader of the Dresden Mission and essentially the leader of the Church in the GDR. As he gave patriarchal blessings, Brother Krause was deeply impressed to promise members the blessings of the temple. Then, in 1975, on a hilltop overlooking the Elbe River, Elder Monson prayed for temple blessings to be given to the faithful German people. This prompted President Burkhardt to increase his efforts in speaking to government officials about the need for the Saints to attend the temple. German members sent in visas hoping to obtain permission to travel to the Switzerland temple.

In 1978, a miracle occurred when President Burkhardt met with the Ministry of Religious Affairs in Berlin. The government leader told him to stop having the Saints send in visas because they would never be allowed to leave. He said, "You have made it abundantly clear

---

164. Boone and Cowan, "The Freiberg Germany Temple."
165. Boone and Cowan, "The Freiberg Germany Temple."

why it is important for your people to attend a temple, but what we do not understand is why your church does not build a temple right here."[166] Suddenly, the Church had permission to build a temple in the GDR! Excited and surprised, Burkhardt informed Elder Monson about this opportunity. A couple of months later, Church leaders drew up plans for a small building to be made for temple worship.

The next step was to determine the location of the temple. After Church leaders failed to receive permission to build in a few cities, the government recommended Freiberg (which means "free mountain," as Boone and Cowan explained)[167] as a potential site. On a hill on the outskirts of Freiberg, President Burkhardt and his administrative secretary, Frank Apel, felt impressed that the temple was meant to be built there. City officials supported the building of the temple, making it possible for the Church to buy the land. City officials also insisted that instead of the Church members adding a temple wing to the existing ward building, an entirely new building should be made for the temple, "a building your members can be proud of."[168]

As the architectural committee drew up plans, the government allowed for a new meetinghouse to be built. Leaders made plans for a temple, a stake center, a dormitory building for temple patrons, and a home for the temple president (just around the corner). On April 23, 1983, the groundbreaking for the temple was held. When a member of the Church Building Department warned Elder Monson to be careful with the groundbreaking shovel, Elder Monson said, "German-made shovels don't break."[169]

During the open house of the Freiberg Temple, almost 90,000 people came to see the temple (about double the population of Freiberg). People were willing to wait in long lines, and five to six thousand people per day showed interest in learning more about the Church. On June 28, 1985, a ceremony for the commemorative cornerstone of the temple took place, with several government officials present. Over the next two days, the temple was dedicated. It was a spiritual and joyful

---

166. Boone and Cowan, "The Freiberg Germany Temple."
167. Boone and Cowan, "The Freiberg Germany Temple."
168. Boone and Cowan, "The Freiberg Germany Temple."
169. Boone and Cowan, "The Freiberg Germany Temple."

event. Henry J. Burkhardt became the first president of the Freiberg Temple.

The building of the Freiberg Temple was truly a miracle. As President Monson said, "Frequently people will ask, 'How has it been possible for the Church to obtain permission to build a temple behind the Iron Curtain?' My feeling is simply that the faith and devotion of our Latter-day Saints in that area brought forth the help of Almighty God and provided for them the eternal blessings which they so richly deserve."[170] I can add my humble testimony that there is a sacred spirit at the Freiberg Temple. The German saints were and are wonderful examples of spiritual strength, faith, and resilience.

---

170. Boone and Cowan, "The Freiberg Germany Temple."

Appendix B
Glossary

Important Terms and Resources Referenced Throughout This Book

Strive: "to devote serious effort or energy, endeavor; to struggle in opposition, contend."[171] I use "strive" throughout the book to emphasize that you don't have to be perfect; you just need to keep trying. Striving means giving your best effort and even struggling before improving. Whenever I use the word *strive* in this book, I want you to remember that your best is enough for the Lord.

Finisher's Letter: At the end of my mission, the mission president asked all of us who were going home to write a letter to our future selves, explaining what we had learned from the mission. Two years after the mission, I received this letter from him. I quote this letter throughout my book because it contains useful spiritual principles and insights based on my experiences.

---

171. *Merriam-Webster.com Dictionary*, s.v. "strive," accessed July 23, 2024, https://www.merriam-webster.com/dictionary/strive.

Tender Mercies Journal: One of my mission journals that I used to record blessings, tender mercies from the Lord, and the positives of each day for eighteen months.

Friend of the Church: An individual who is receiving lessons from the missionaries.

Transfer: A six-week period in the mission where you are living in a specific area with a specific companion; after the six weeks, as a missionary, you may get called to a new area or be assigned a new companion

Trainee: A brand-new missionary; in the first two transfers of their mission, they receive extra training from a companion, the "trainer."

Street Displays: In my mission, a term meaning when missionaries, and sometimes members in the area, set up a table with Church materials, scriptures, and so on and try to talk to everyone on the street who passes them.

District: A group of missionaries assigned to an area within a zone.

District Meeting: Frequent meetings between missionaries who serve in the same district or area.

Zone: An area in the mission field that is comprised of multiple districts.

Zone Training Meeting: A meeting held every three months with multiple districts, under the direction of the mission president.

Joint Teaches: When a member goes with you to teach a lesson to a friend of the Church, known as "member lessons" in some missions.

Tschüss Buch: This term literally means "bye book." Our mission and others have a tradition of missionaries printing off pictures and writing letters in each other's "goodbye books," or missionary scrapbooks.

Acknowledgments

I'm extremely grateful for all the help and support I've received as I've embarked on my author journey. If you are a newbie writer, too, know that there are many people willing to help and many resources available.

Thank you to the LDSPMA organization for being an amazing source of knowledge! I'm grateful for the yearly conferences, with its classes and amazing speakers, and the combination of spiritual, literary, and business learning. I'm also grateful for the sense of community in LDSPMA, for the online zoom lectures, and for kind mentors who freely share their talents and skills.

Thank you to my husband, Bryce, for being the one to tell me, "just do it." Thanks for helping me pick a date to finish my manuscript by and for believing in me and supporting me. I love you!

Thank you to my mother, Lisa, and my sister-in-law, Bre, for reading my book and being supportive every step of the way. I appreciate your enthusiasm, your words of encouragement, and for always validating me and my story.

Thank you to my brother, Noah, for his support with my book and helping me with my social media accounts. Thanks for always answering my frequent, frantic texts and reassuring me about my posts and stories! You are my social media expert.

A huge thank you to my beta readers for their support and helpful feedback! My book would be in rough shape without you. Thank you for your insights, expertise, and for catching things I missed: Shellie, Annika, McKinsey, Bre, and Peter.

Thank you to my family and friends for being interested in my book. Thank you for supporting me!

And thank you to the Spanish Fork Library for being the best place to get work done!

I'd also like to give a shout-out to my dad, Jesse, for his inspiring counsel on my mission. Thank you to all my companions, the ward members in Germany, my ward and mission leaders, and friends of the Church for being a part of my life-changing missionary experience. Thank you to both friends and strangers who showed me kindness and who share God's love with all.

Thank you for the team at Cedar Fort and a huge thank you to my editor, Liz, for believing in my book and going above and beyond as an editor. Thank you for making my dream of getting my book published a reality!

About the Author

Hannah served a mission for The Church of Jesus Christ of Latter-day Saints in Germany. Not only did she enjoy touring castles and eating delicious chocolate, but she grew spiritually and learned about charity and faith from the examples of members, friends, and fellow missionaries. Hannah has written a book about her experience with the hope of helping other young women be more prepared than she was and empowered to serve with confidence.

After her missionary service, Hannah graduated from Brigham Young University with a bachelor's degree in English and German and a master's degree in sociology. She loves school so much that she decided to become a professor, and she teaches sociology classes at a local community college. In her spare time, Hannah loves writing, running, pretending to be a mermaid, and going on fun adventures with her husband.

Scan to visit

https://hannahshoafhardy.com/